The editor

Clare Hanson is Lecturer in English at the
College of St. Paul and St. Mary,
Cheltenham, Gloucestershire. Her previous
publications include *Katherine Mansfield*
(with Andrew Gurr) and *Short Stories and
Short Fictions, 1880–1980*.

THE CRITICAL WRITINGS OF KATHERINE MANSFIELD

Also by Clare Hanson

KATHERINE MANSFIELD (*with Andrew Gurr*)

SHORT STORIES AND SHORT FICTIONS, 1880–1980

The Critical Writings of Katherine Mansfield

Edited and introduced by

Clare Hanson
Lecturer in English
College of St. Paul and St. Mary, Cheltenham

St. Martin's Press   New York

First published in the United States of America in 1987

Printed in Hong Kong

ISBN 0–312–17514–0

Library of Congress Cataloging-in-Publication Data
Mansfield, Katherine, 1888–1923.
The critical writings of Katherine Mansfield.
Bibliography: p.
Includes index.
I. Hanson, Clare.   II. Title.
PR9639.3.M258A6   1987   823'.912   86–15464
ISBN 0–312–17514–0

Contents

87–24366

Preface

The term 'critical writings' is a wide one, but has been chosen for the title of this book for precisely that reason. Unlike many writers – Joyce, for example, or Lawrence – Katherine Mansfield kept a 'journal' throughout her writing life (although in the form of irregular notebook jottings, not as the monolithic daily record suggested by Murry's introductions to the 1927 and 1954 *Journals*). KM confided many of her most interesting comments on her art to her 'unseen, unknown companion', as she called her notebooks. She also put an unusual degree of creative and critical energy into the letters she wrote to John Middleton Murry, which were, in the special circumstances of her illness and isolation, literally a lifeline to her. For this reason it is more than usually difficult to draw a line around KM's 'critical writings' and to separate her formal and informal reflections on her art. In preparing this edition I have therefore garnered material from her letters and journals as well as from formal reviews and essays. While emphasising the importance of the body of formal criticism KM produced for the *Athenaeum*, I would wish this criticism to be seen in the wider context which letter and journal material can provide.

In selecting from a mass of material I have been guided above all by considerations of critical relevance. In the case of letter and journal material, selection is made easy by the clarity and lucidity of KM's own mind and writing. In the case of the reviews, where she was to a considerable degree oppressed by the hand of convention, selection of material became more difficult. I have finally decided to omit all *Athenaeum* reviews of inferior novelists which did not spark off a significant reaction in KM herself. I have also omitted those parts of reviews where KM, according to the critical fashion of her day, simply retells the story of a novel. I have tried, too, not to duplicate material.

I hope that this new edition of her critical writings will both win new readers for KM as critic, and suggest different perspectives for those already familiar with such criticism as has previously been published in letter and journal selections.

C.H.

Acknowledgements

In preparing this edition I have incurred many debts. I am grateful to Anthony Alpers, for a brief but decisive telephone conversation which provided many 'leads'; to Ian Gordon for practical help during the period when I was working on Katherine Mansfield in Wellington; to C. K. Stead for his insights into the peculiar difficulties of KM's position as a writer–critic in exile. I am indebted to Margaret Scott for her confirmation of some difficult readings from KM's notebooks, and to Vincent O'Sullivan for useful discussions on KM's life and work.

I am grateful also to the Research Board of the University of Reading for a grant which enabled me to travel to New Zealand to study KM's manuscripts, and to the College of St Paul and St Mary, Cheltenham, for further generous research assistance.

The Alexander Turnbull Library, Wellington, and the British Museum have kindly allowed me to use material in their possession. I should like to thank the Society of Authors as the literary representative of the estate of Katherine Mansfield, for permission to quote from published and unpublished writings which are still in copyright. I should also like to thank Random House Inc. and Alfred A. Knopf Inc. for permission to reprint the extracts from the *Journal of Katherine Mansfield*, copyright 1927 by Alfred A. Knopf Inc. and renewed 1955 by J. Middleton Murry, and for permission to reprint the extracts from *The Letters of Katherine Mansfield*, ed. John Middleton Murry, copyright 1929 by Alfred A. Knopf Inc. and renewed 1957 by J. Middleton Murry.

A Note on Sources

The principal source for the material in this edition is the periodical the *Athenaeum* for the years 1919–20. All the *Athenaeum* reviews printed here have been checked against the original periodical issues, and inaccuracies in John Middleton Murry's transcriptions of the reviews for his edition of *Novels and Novelists* (1930) have been corrected. The second major source of material is Katherine Mansfield's letters to Murry, which have also been checked against the manuscript originals held by the Alexander Turnbull Library, and, where necessary, emended.

In view of the essential soundness of Murry's transcriptions from KM's manuscripts, material from his 1928 edition of her letters and 1954 edition of her journal has been allowed to stand. In the case of the letters, it seemed unnecessary to duplicate the labours of Vincent O'Sullivan and Margaret Scott, currently transcribing and editing the collected letters of KM; similarly, in the case of the so-called journal material, it seemed unnecessary to attempt another transcription in the light of the probable publication in full of KM's notebooks in the near future. However, wherever letter or journal material in this edition is cited as previously unpublished, the transcription is my own, from manuscript originals.

Introduction

'Not being an intellectual', Katherine Mansfield wrote to John Middleton Murry in 1920, 'I always seem to have to learn things at the risk of my life.' The remark suggests some of the dangers inherent in the enterprise of attempting to establish KM's reputation as a critic. She is alluding here, with some hostility, to Murry's book of critical essays *The Evolution of an Intellectual* (1920), and distancing herself from the kind of professional criticism produced by Murry, which did not often represent something learnt 'at the risk of [one's] life'. In an earlier letter she expressed her distaste for Murry's intellectual approach: a note of conviction is sustained rather than undermined by her admission of feelings of vulnerability in writing as a (relatively) uneducated woman and as a colonial – the 'little Colonial' from Karori.

> But this intellectual reasoning is never *the whole truth*. It's not *the artist's truth* – not *creative*. If man were an intellect it would do, but man ISN'T. Now I must be fair, I must be fair. Who am I to be certain that I understand? There's always Karori to shout after me. *Shout* it.[1]

From such a perspective KM's formal critical writings might be seen as anomalous: it could be argued that the reviews she wrote in 1919 and 1920 for the *Athenaeum*, in particular, were written against the grain, from a desire to placate Murry. Yet KM put 'her all' into these reviews, and devoted nearly two years of her short writing life to them, at the expense of her fiction. While we must acknowledge the reservations she felt about formal literary criticism and the English upper-middle-class male values embodied in it, we must recognise too that her critical writings represent a genuine attempt to take on the literary establishment on its own terms. KM wanted to 'preach',[2] to convert, and could and would take up the opposition's weapons in order to do this. The extent to which she at the same time subverted and undercut contemporary literary-critical forms must by the same token be recognised.

KM's critical writings are not well known (unlike those of Virginia Woolf, for example), and it has been suggested that her finest critical insights came in an impromptu fashion, and were dashed off in moments of inspiration in letters and journals. This rather romantic view both fosters and depends on an over-emphasis on the immediately accessible 'personality' of the author, which, it is supposed, is reflected in all her writings. For the purpose of this introduction I would like to shift attention away from the attractive personality of 'Katherine Mansfield', back to the writing, in this case that body of critical work which lies so solidly across the path of the would-be KM reader or critic. What meaning, and what status, should we assign to it?

The difficulties of decision in this particular case are compounded by the presence of J. M. Murry in KM's life as in her work. Murry acted as KM's agent and took responsibility for the publication of her life and writings in a process of re-presentation which began years before her death. Anthony Alpers has suggested that Murry introduced a kind of 'fuzziness' into the public picture of KM.[3] Certainly there is an unmistakable preference for the softer focus and rosier hue in Murry's view, as is suggested in Lytton Strachey's acid summing up of the discrepancy between the portrait of a lady produced for the public in Murry's 1927 *Journal*, and the woman he thought he had known: 'But why that foul-mouthed, virulent, brazen-faced broomstick of a creature should have got herself up as a pad of rose-scented cotton wool is beyond me', he wrote.[4]

For a variety of perfectly understandable reasons it would seem that Murry frequently miscast and misread KM both as a person and as a writer. At the very beginning of their relationship KM *wrote* to him (significantly) about her loathing of the role of 'wife':

> Yes, I hate hate *hate* doing these things that you accept just as all men accept of their women. I can only play the servant with a very bad grace indeed. It's all very well for females who have nothing else to do ...[5]

Eight years later, still in the same vein, she wrote of Murry's refusal to accept the fact that for her, as for Virginia Woolf, the roles of 'wife' and 'writer' were – not just because of illness – incompatible:

> My only trouble is John. He ought to divorce me, marry a really young healthy creature, have children and ask me to be godmother. I shall never be a wife and I feel such a fraud when he believes that one day I shall turn into one.[6]

Murry's failures of vision affected important areas of professional life: it was while he was acting as KM's literary agent, for example, that he released what Anthony Alpers calls the 'detested 1913 photograph' for publicity purposes. The photograph was rejected by KM not just because it gave a false picture of her as brimming with rude health, but because it gave a misleading picture of her *as a woman* and/or as a writer. KM complained too, when *Bliss, and Other Stories* was published, about what she perceived as a conflict inherent in the presentation of 'Katherine Mansfield' both as a woman and a writer. She felt threatened with silence specifically because of this conflict:

> Just while I'm on the subject I suppose you will think I am an egocentric to mind the way Constable has advertised my book and the paragraph that is on the paper cover. I'd like to say that I mind so terribly that there are no words for me. No – I'm DUMB!! I think it so insulting and disgusting and undignified that – well – there you are! It's no good suffering all over again. But the bit about 'Women will learn by heart and not repeat'. Gods! why didn't they have a photograph of me looking through a garter. But I was helpless here – too late to stop it – so now I *must* prove – no, convince people ce n'est pas moi. At least, if I'd known they were going to say that, no power on earth would have made me cut a word. I wish I hadn't. I was wrong – very wrong.[7]

To come down to more tangible textual matters, it is clear that Murry had a hand in the bowdlerisation of KM's fiction as well as of her letters and journals. In the quotation above, KM is referring to the fact that 'Je ne parle pas français' (one of the only two stories, she said in 1922, that satisfied her to any extent) had been adulterated for its publication by Constable. The original text, as published by the Heron Press in 1919, is far bolder – the story ends, for example, with two additional paragraphs:

I must go. I must go. I reach down my coat and hat. Madame knows me. 'You haven't dined yet?' she smiles.

'No, not yet, Madame.' [Constable text ends here.]

I'd rather like to dine with her. Even to sleep with her afterwards. Would she be pale like that all over?

But no. She'd have large moles. They go with that kind of skin. And I can't bear them. They remind me somehow, disgustingly, of mushrooms.[8]

Many references to sexuality (important for the particular kind of 'corruption' KM was evoking here) have been cut for the Constable edition: KM felt she had 'picked the eyes out of [her] story', at Murry's and Michael Sadleir's instigation, to ensure its publication. Of course, she was responding to social pressures, not only to Murry, in doing this, and it would be wrong to suggest that Murry should take sole responsibility for the ways in which his wife's work and personality were presented to the public. It is unfair, I think, to take the line taken by Leonard Woolf, who claimed that Murry had a malevolent influence on KM which was in some way outside her control:

I think that in some abstruse way Murry corrupted and perverted and destroyed Katherine both as a person and a writer. . . . She got enmeshed in the sticky sentimentality of Murry and wrote against the grain of her own nature.[9]

But Murry did certainly suggest, during KM's lifetime, that she should hide some of her cutting edge from the public, and after her death he ensured that her sharpness did not often appear. He was far more concerned than KM with the question of what it was decorous for a woman writer to say, and the effect of his editing of KM's life and works has undoubtedly been to obscure the clarity, the harshness and, I would suggest, the more 'masculine' qualities of her mind.

In KM's critical writings Murry's influence is directly detectable in certain turns of phrase and in a kind of portentousness which appears particularly in the earlier reviews. KM and Murry wrote enthusiastic manifesto articles together for *Rhythm* in 1912, and something of the Murry tone still lingers in the first reviews KM wrote for the *Athenaeum* – in the closing lines of a review of Maugham's *The Moon and Sixpence*, for example:

But great artists are not drunken men; they are men who are divinely sober. They know that the moon can never be bought for sixpence, and that liberty is only a profound realisation of the greatness of the dangers in their midst.[10]

But KM quickly pulled herself up: she commented crisply when she pasted this review into her notebook, 'Shows traces of hurry & at the end, is pompous!'[11]

Her achievement was precisely to create her own voice – the least portentous of voices – while working within many constraints, both in the *Athenaeum* reviews and in her critical writing in letters and journals. Seen in this context, of an achieved critical point of view, Murry's influence (apart from specific questions of style or tone) is perhaps best seen as symbolic – he acts as a convenient scapegoat, a representative of many of the values of the contemporary literary establishment which KM wished to resist.

What KM really wanted to do in her criticism is explained in a letter of 1920 in which she admonished Murry regarding the *Athenaeum*:

In my reckless way I would suggest all reviews were signed and all were put into the first person. I think that would give the whole paper an amazing lift-up. A paper that length must be *definite, personal* or die. It can't afford the 'we' – 'in our opinion'. To sign reviews, to put them in the 1st person stimulates curiosity, *makes for correspondence*, gives it (to be 19-eleventyish[12]) GUTS. You see it's a case of leaning out of a window with a board and a nail, *or a bouquet, or* a flag – administering whichever it is and retiring *sharp*. This seems to me essential.[13]

It is tempting to suggest that KM's dislike of the impersonal third-person style of contemporary reviewing is distinctively 'feminine', and on these grounds to align her with a writer such as Dorothy Richardson, who was a conscious campaigner against the rigid, impersonal, rule-bound qualities of 'male prose'. Yet this would be misleading and the adoption of such convenient distinctions might obscure the real complexity of KM's position as a woman writer at a particular point in time, writing for a particular audience. It does not take much reflection to see, for example, that KM's writing, both creative and critical, has qualities which, in such terms, would have to be considered 'masculine', though it is also true that it is very difficult to determine when she is consciously cultivating a 'masculine' tone for defensive purposes.

In broad terms, KM wanted her criticism to be more personal, and more concrete, very much as she wished her fiction to be 'personal'[14] and concretely affective, and she adopted rather similar strategies to achieve this. She sought the freedom of a tone in which she could be, as far as that was possible, 'most herself, and least personal', a tone achieved through placing of the self in a dramatic context and through the use of symbolism and indirect allusion rather than direct statement. She adopted a persona in her criticism just as she did in her fiction: a persona which is androgynous – tough, 'masculine' and fearless on the one hand, yet capable of the finest (feminine) judgements and discriminations on the other. A prevailing note of irony dissolves tensions between male and female, writer and work: we can see such irony in operation, defusing potentially disabling oppositions, in this extract from a review of M. Austen-Leigh's *Personal Aspects of Jane Austen*:

> It seems almost unkind to criticise a little book which has thrown on bonnet and shawl and tripped across the fields of criticism at so round a pace to defend its dear Jane Austen. . . . Can we picture Jane Austen caring – except in a delightfully wicked way which we are sure the author of this book would not allow – that people said she was no lady, was not fond of children, hated animals, did not care a pin for the poor, could not have written about foreign parts if she had tried, had no idea how a fox was killed, but rather thought it ran up a tree and hissed at the hound at the last – was, in short, cold, coarse, practically illiterate and without morality? Mightn't her reply have been, 'Ah, but what about my novels?'[15]

KM's criticism is also marked, like that of her modernist contemporaries Woolf and Eliot, by a striking and vivid use of metaphor. Such criticism is often called 'impressionistic' – the term has been applied particularly often to the sometimes flamboyant criticism of Virginia Woolf. Yet KM's literary criticism is the reverse of impressionistic in the derogatory sense of diffuse or vague. Through the use of metaphor she achieves two major objectives.

First, she enforces an extension of our critical capacity – we are led into an acknowledgement of relationships and suggestive analogies of whose existence we had previously been unaware. And it is important to note that in this context, of a discourse of persuasion, metaphor works very much as it does in some metaphysical poetry, to evoke and create very precise images and qualities.

Secondly, however, KM is able to exploit the 'luminous halo' surrounding the lighted core of any given metaphor: she is able to utilise the wider, less well defined attributes or associations of a particular image in order to suggest indirectly a point of view which she was unable openly to state. This kind of 'secondary' indirection is particularly important when we are considering the formal, and, in some respects, restrictive context in which the *Athenaeum* reviews were written. To take an example, in her review of Virginia Woolf's *Night and Day*, KM is able through her use of the metaphor of the ship for this novel to bring to our notice not only its solid, craftsman-like qualities and its seriousness (it is or it has been launched on the sea, which serves KM again and again as a metaphor for knowledge, consciousness and discovery), but also its heaviness and its rather unyielding aspects. These qualities of the ship are actually foregrounded by KM as she develops the metaphor:

> To us who love to linger down at the harbour, as it were, watching the new ships being builded, the old ones returning, and the many putting out to sea, comes the strange sight of *Night and Day* sailing into port serene and resolute on a deliberate wind. The strangeness lies in her aloofness, her air of quiet perfection, her lack of any sign that she has made a perilous voyage – the absence of any scars. There she lies among the strange shipping – a tribute to civilisation for our admiration and wonder.[16]

KM similarly uses an extended metaphor in order briskly to dispose of Mrs Wharton:

> But what about us? What about her readers? Does Mrs Wharton expect us to grow warm in a gallery where the temperature is so sparklingly cool? We are looking at portraits – are we not? These are human beings, arranged for exhibition purposes, framed, glazed, and hung in the perfect light. They pale, they grow paler, they flush, they raise their 'clearest eyes', they hold out their arms to each other 'extended, but not rigid', and the voice is the voice of the portrait.[17]

KM's use of metaphor in her critical writings is thus not only a matter of personal preference in the sense that she was (or, rather, had become) a symbolist writer, delighting in obliquity and 'fine shades': it also served a very definite tactical purpose, enabling her to be 'definite and personal' in her criticism despite the constraints and conventions of her medium.

Other strategies employed by KM to subvert critical forms from within include the impassive retelling of a story simply in order to make it ridiculous. The tone of many of the novel reviews reminds us of Leonard Woolf's memorable picture of KM:

> I don't think anyone has ever made me laugh more than she did in those days. She would sit very upright on the edge of a chair or sofa and tell at immense length a kind of saga of her experiences as an actress or of how and why Koteliansky howled like a dog in the room at the top of the building in Southampton Row. There was not the shadow of a gleam of a smile on her mask of a face, and the extraordinary funniness of the story was increased by the flashes of her astringent wit.[18]

Another tactic KM often adopts is the use of a rhetorical question to open a review, and then of a suspended conclusion – the effect is that of disclaiming responsibility for the criticism which has just been produced. An example is 'Anodyne', a withering account of a 'pastime novel', which opens with the bland question, 'What is a "sweetly pretty" novel?' and ends, 'though you would not doubt the issue of the fight, you cannot be absolutely certain how the victory will be obtained, and so – you read on'. At the end of the review KM is, as it were, like the cat which has neatly regained its balance after performing a superb trick – and then, like Kezia in 'Prelude', tiptoes away.

II

So KM, working flexibly within cultural and social restrictions and conventions, manages to a considerable extent to fit her own prescription and to be 'definite and personal' in her criticism. In looking more closely at this criticism it is useful, if rather artificial, to make a distinction between its general interest and value and its particular relevance for a consideration of KM's own fiction. In making high claims for her literary criticism, one is by implication inviting a reassessment of her creative work. I suggest that this is especially important in the case of KM, for in her work, as in that of many modernist writers, there is a particularly close connection between critical and creative writing. Modernist literature is by its nature oblique, allusive, formally experimental, and may exhibit a certain logical discontinuity. Most modernist writers have in consequence found it necessary to prepare and create the audience for their work, explaining their aims and techniques in critical manifestos which have acted as glosses on their work. Examples are T. S. Eliot's essays in the *Criterion*, or Virginia Woolf's early essays. I would suggest that the fiction of KM, too, would benefit from being read in the light of her expressed aesthetic aims, and that such a reading would lead to a fuller understanding and appreciation of her allusive and elusive art.

In order to understand KM's 'personal' aesthetic in this sense – her *particular* aims as a writer – we must focus predominantly on her technical and practical remarks on writing, more evident in the letters and journals, as we would expect, than in the formal reviews. The most important aspect of KM's aesthetic to emerge from such scrutiny is its symbolist[19] bias. KM was a symbolist writer in the sense that her work belongs to the post-Symbolist tradition in European literature. KM's earliest literary mentors were Arthur Symons and Oscar Wilde, the two most important representatives or 'translators' of the French Symbolist movement. KM's familiarity with the work of Symons, in particular, becomes clear from a study of her early – previously unpublished – notes on his work, printed in Appendix 1; Wilde too appears frequently in the early notebooks as a tutelary figure. The central idea which she took from these writers was the belief that in literature abstract states of mind or feeling should be conveyed through concrete images rather than described analytically. This view is expressed with remarkable clarity in an early notebook entry which appears among her annotations of Symons's *Studies in Prose and Verse*[20] (1904):

The partisans of analysis describe minutely the state of the soul; the secret motive of every action as being of far greater importance than the action itself. The partisans of objectivity – give us the result of this evolution sans describing the secret processes. They describe the state of the soul through the slightest gesture – i.e. realise flesh covered bones – which is the artist's method for me –

in as much as art seems to me *pure vision* – I am indeed a partisan of objectivity –[21]

It is a view to which KM held throughout her career. Compare, for example, this 1919 letter to Murry on her own indirect method in fiction (she is writing about the effect of the war on her contemporaries):

> I can't imagine how after the war these men can pick up the old threads as though it had never been. Speaking to *you* I'd say we have died and live again. How can that be the same life? It doesn't mean that life is the less precious or that the 'common things of light and day' are gone. They are not gone, they are intensified, they are illumined. Now we know ourselves for what we are. In a way it's a tragic knowledge. . . .
>
> But, of course, you don't imagine I mean by this knowledge let-us-eat-and-drinkism. No, I mean 'deserts of vast eternity'. But the difference between you and me is (perhaps I'm wrong) I couldn't tell anybody *bang out* about those deserts; they are my secret. I might write about a boy eating strawberries or a woman combing her hair on a windy morning, and that is the only way I can ever mention them. But they *must* be there. Nothing less will do.[22]

An abstract theme must be suggested through concrete images and symbols, and thus returned to its origin in concrete experience. Thus, in a Mansfield story, we might expect to find that most of the 'narrative' details work in this way, having a symbolic as well as a narrative function: in this respect her work may be closely linked with that of Joyce (of whom, incidentally, she could not conceivably have been aware in 1908, the date of the notebook entry on the revelation of the soul 'through the slightest gesture'). Both writers – independently – effected a revolution in the short-story form by introducing into it techniques of systematic allusion derived ultimately from French Symbolist poetry.

There is a limit, however, to the extent to which the all-purpose label 'symbolist' will fit KM. In one important respect her aesthetic differs from that of the symbolists: it is a difference that by its nature becomes clearer if we look beyond KM's letters and journal to her formal critical writing. A belief strongly expressed in the reviews is that art has an ethical *dimension*, if not an ethical function: KM did not in this respect assent to the symbolist belief in art as an entirely autotelic activity. While she did not suggest that the artist should in any crude sense set out to preach or prove a point, she did believe that the 'true' artist's work would make an ethical 'impression', and that it was the duty of the critic to register this impression and measure its depth and quality. This is a role which she plays, in the least abrasive manner, in much of her critical writing – for example, in a 1920 review of Galsworthy's *In Chancery*, in which she laments his inability to regard his characters 'from an eminence' both moral and intellectual:

> It is a very great gift for an author to be able to project himself into the hearts and minds of his characters – but more is needed to make a great creative artist: he must be able, with equal power, to withdraw, to survey what is happening – and from an eminence.[23]

While noting this 'ethical' aspect of KM's aesthetic, however, it is important too to observe the almost Jamesian distinctions which she herself made about the scope and function of the ethical element in art. She explains her position most clearly in a journal note on the philosophy of Vaihinger. Here she asserts the intrinsic identity of ethical and aesthetic ends ('the ideal') but suggests that this ideality can, paradoxically, only be achieved *within* the work of art itself, removed from *practical* use and function:

> Reality cannot become the ideal, the dream; and it is not the business of the artist to grind an axe, to try to impose his vision of life upon the existing world. Art is not an attempt of the artist to reconcile existence with his vision; it is an attempt to create his own world *in* this world.[24]

The second major aspect of KM's 'personal' aesthetic is her emphasis on memory, which she places at the centre of the artistic process. Memory is both selective, isolating the salient features of a particular event or experience, and synthetic, superimposing and juxtaposing remembered scenes and images so that in time (in the fullest sense) experience is literally reconstituted. This process is not mechanical but organic, and it too has an ethical[25] dimension which is rooted in the individual artist's temperament and disposition. These beliefs are expressed most forcefully in the review of Dorothy

Richardson's *The Tunnel* which opened KM's series of reviews for the *Athenaeum*. Here, the moral and idealising aspects of memory are evoked through apocalyptic imagery:

> There is one who could not live in so tempestuous an environment as her mind – and he is Memory. She has no memory. It is true that Life is sometimes very swift and breathless, but not always. If we are to be truly alive there are large pauses in which we creep away into our caves of contemplation. And then it is, in the silence, that Memory mounts his throne and judges all that is in our minds – appointing each his separate place, high or low, rejecting this, selecting that – putting this one to shine in the light and throwing that one into the darkness.
>
> We do not mean to say that those large, round biscuits might not be in the light, or the night in Spring be in the darkness. Only we feel that until these things are judged and given each its appointed place in the whole scheme, they have no meaning in the world of art.[26]

Memory idealises, in the fullest sense, and makes (ethical) judgements and discriminations; it is important to recognise this element in KM's richly worked and polished fiction, which is 'slight' or 'episodic' only in the most nominal technical sense.

III

Besides shedding light on KM's own aims and achievement in fiction, her criticism has an interest and value which extends far beyond particular insights into contemporary writers. The formal reviews written for the *Athenaeum* (as opposed to the working-notes found in letters and journals) constitute a formidable body of criticism, a framework of (sometimes veiled) polemic and advocacy. It has already been indicated that one of the important themes of KM's criticism is that of the effects of the First World War: this is partly a simple function of the timing of the reviewing-stint, but also stems from KM's clear belief that the war had, or should have, entirely changed man's perception of himself. She wrote to Murry that 'we have to face our war', the implication being that artists could not dismiss the war as the responsibility of other people, as many, she felt, wished to do. While illness made KM particularly susceptible to intimations of frailty and mortality associated with the war, one cannot deny the justice of her charge that for many artists the war simply had not been 'felt'. For most, direct personal suffering had been avoided, and the war had not brought a greater consciousness of man's inhumanity to man. When KM wrote that as a result of the war 'now we know ourselves for what we are', she was speaking, she felt, for a tiny minority – a minority which included most notably D. H. Lawrence (see KM's note on *Aaron's Rod*, 1922).

The major thrust of KM's polemic in the *Athenaeum* reviews is in an area related to her feelings about the war: she was concerned above all with 'seriousness in art', concerned that the literature of her day should, using whatever techniques were necessary, address the deeper issues of life – 'nothing less will do'. She felt that much of the fiction she encountered was trivial, and consequently her attempts at definition of what is worthwhile in art occur as frequently in a context of denunciation (for instance, of the third-rate novels of Gilbert Cannan, or of the 'pastime novel') as in one of admiration and congratulation. Like all reviewers, KM was deluged with inferior novels: what makes her outstanding as a critic is the deft and deadly way in which she analyses the failures she so often encounters and, more rarely, illuminates the successful, achieved work of art.

It is important in this context to point out that KM was writing for the *Athenaeum* in a period which appeared a desert in terms of fiction: as Anthony Alpers has remarked,[27] reading the *Athenaeum* reviews one comes fully to appreciate the climate of mingled dearth and expectation in which *The Garden Party, Jacob's Room* and *Ulysses* were so rapturously received. It was a desert more apparent than real, as Lawrence, Joyce, KM and Woolf were all writing in the years before 1922 – but were not, for a variety of reasons, being published. Compared to the dramatic developments taking place in visual art at the same time, literature seemed to be lagging dully behind.

It is fortunate that KM was able with such frequency to turn reviews of novels which disappointed her into occasions for the exploration and celebration of those qualities which make for distinction. In a review of Joseph Hergesheimer's *Linda Condon*, for example, she uses the Yeatsian image of the tree to suggest the organic wholeness of the successful work of art – *not* achieved in this particular instance:

> If a novel is to have a central idea we imagine that central idea is a lusty growing stem from which the branches spring clothed with leaves, and the buds become flowers and fruits. We imagine that the author chooses with infinite deliberation the very air in which that tree shall be nourished, and that he is profoundly aware that its coming to perfection depends upon the strength with which the central idea supports its beautiful accumulations.[28]

The extended metaphor is one of the most often used tools through which she places, though often in negative terms, moral and aesthetic qualities. So, to register just a few, she uses metaphors for familiarity and change (the shallow and the deeper seas, the known and the unknown hotel); employs consumer metaphors for fictions which are no more than conventional confections or 'digestible snacks',[29] uses 'artful' metaphors for artful novels where the characters resemble portraits hanging in a gallery; or evokes in detail the atmosphere of the 'Garden City novel' with homes 'which seem to breathe white enamel and cork linoleum and the works of Freud and Jung'.[30]

As these allusions should make sufficiently clear, it is extremely difficult to disentangle ethical and aesthetic motives and beliefs in KM's literary criticism. It may be useful here to make a distinction between the 'ethical' and the 'moral': 'moral' might be used to refer to the practical sphere, to matters of action and conduct, while 'ethical' would denote a more disinterested ethical sense, rather like the 'undestroyed freshness' of Maisie in James's *What Maisie Knew*, which is, as it were, as much a matter of taste as of judgement. It is in this light – in relation to the 'ethical' in this sense – that we can perhaps best see KM's insistence on the relation between the ethical and the aesthetic, and on the relation between 'life' and 'art'. It is by no means a naïve insistence. In, for example, a review of *Mary Olivier: A Life* by May Sinclair, KM uses Blake's image of the 'bounding line' to suggest that widest possible ethical and aesthetic perspective which, she felt, should distinguish the great novel (and which was of course lacking in Sinclair's work):

But if the Flood, the sky, the rainbow, or what Blake beautifully calls the bounding outline, be removed and if, further, no one thing is to be related to another thing, we do not see what is to prevent the whole of mankind turning author.

She goes on:

Is it not the great abiding satisfaction of a work of art that the writer was master of the situation when he wrote it and at the mercy of nothing less mysterious than a greater work of art?[31]

The suggestion that the world of art and the world of 'fact' are analogous and conterminous (it is the world itself which is of course the greater work of art) reflects KM's very modernist feeling for the unreality and insubstantiality of any external world conceived of as existing outside the (involuntarily) creative mind of man.

To move now to – in relative terms – more specific issues, KM's criticism is of interest in relation to two questions much debated at the time: the influence of Russian literature in England between 1900 and 1920, and the contemporary debate over 'feminine prose'. KM was in a special position in relation to Russian literature. She felt passionately about it, as is indicated in this 1919 letter to Koteliansky:

When you think that the english [*sic*] literary world is given up to sniggerers, dishonesty, sneering *dull*, *dull* giggling at Victorians in side-whiskers and here is this treasure – at the wharf only not unloaded . . . I feel that Art is like a sick person, left all alone in a house where they are having a jazz party downstairs and we have at least something of what that sick person needs to be well again. Can't we thieve up the back staircase and take it?[32]

She shares the general contemporary enthusiasm for Russian literature, and sense of its pre-eminence, but, perhaps because she worked intensively on translations from the Russian in collaboration with Koteliansky, she had a more acute, if sometimes frustrated, sense than most of the specificity of the achievement of the great Russian writers. Her method in translation was to work from Koteliansky's strange but literal translations, re-creating, in so far as she could, the sense of the original, and restoring harmony to the splintered fragments of Koteliansky's prose. The process taught her enough about the Russian language for her to feel confident in criticising Constance Garnett's (very influential) translations: she wrote in another 1919 letter to Koteliansky, 'She [Garnett] seems to take the nerve out of Chekhov before she starts working on him, like the dentist takes the nerve from a tooth.'

The most intriguing question, in this context, is that of KM's reaction to the work of Chekhov, whose work she has so often been accused of plagiarising. It is quite clear from an examination of KM's early notebooks that she had developed her method of obliquity and indirection quite independently of any study which she may have made of the works of Chekhov, and her attitude in her critical writings – formal and informal – is in every way consistent with this fact. Her attitude is one of joyful celebration, and there is no sign of the grudging or awkward praise which we would expect if she were dealing with an author towards whom she had an 'unholy' obligation.

There are two key reviews in relation to Chekhov. The first is the unsigned review of *The Cherry Orchard*, collected here for the first time. The review is remarkable more for its sensitivity to Chekhov's dramatic method, and its awareness of the implications of his work for the form of drama as a whole, than for its insight into the particular themes of this play. I would suggest that this fact, taken together with the way in which the review tails off into repetition and generalisation, indicates that it was in fact written jointly (and hurriedly) with Murry[33] – Murry finishing the review while KM had barely begun to make her points about the play.

The other review in which KM discusses Chekhov is that entitled 'Wanted, a New World' (25 June 1920). The books ostensibly under consideration here are three collections of 'short stories' or 'tales', as KM variously calls them. KM takes the opportunity that the contrasting failure of these stories afforded her to discuss the achievement of Chekhov. The review is significant because it is one of the very few in which she discusses directly the short-story form. In it she aligns herself with Chekhov as the pioneer of an art which she can only define negatively, *against* conventional terms and forms – 'I am neither a short story, nor a sketch, nor an impression, nor a tale', she writes. The missing term we might supply here is 'short fiction', to denote that kind of short prose fiction produced first by Chekhov and then by KM, in which action is less important than atmosphere and in which the process of language tends increasingly to become part of the subject as well as the agent of composition (this type of short fiction has been developed most notably by Beckett in English fiction).

KM's relation to another contentious contemporary issue, that of 'feminine prose', is in itself contentious, or adversarial. Whether by design on Murry's part or not, KM did the bulk of the reviewing of novels by women during the period when she was with the *Athenaeum*. Her reviews thus offer an original response to the work of many women writers who are currently being reinstated in the literary canon: for example, May Sinclair, Rose Macaulay, Rhoda Broughton, Sheila Kaye-Smith. On the whole KM is more lenient with these writers than with their male counterparts (compare for example the review of Sheila Kaye-Smith's *Tamarisk Town* with that of Hugh Walpole's *The Captives*); it is correspondingly true that by implication she takes male writers such as Walpole more seriously. Even more striking is the fact that she comes out very firmly against those women writers who were at this time attempting to pioneer a 'feminine prose'. I would suggest that, to some extent, her attacks on writers such as May Sinclair and Dorothy Richardson were defensive rather than offensive, and that her wariness of their fiction stems from the fact that it pointed to a whole area which was problematic and unresolved for her.

Elaine Showalter, in *A Literature of their Own*, sets the scene for a consideration of 'feminine prose'; she points out that by 1920 the debate over this issue was in full swing – R. Brimley Johnson, for example, had just produced a critical study in which he attempted to define the qualities of 'the new female version of realism'. He singled out May Sinclair's claim (in *The Creators*, 1910) that experience (in the sense of incident or adventure) can only hinder the woman writer: Showalter rightly links this with Sinclair's 'charmed' response to the work of Richardson – 'Nothing happens. It just goes on and on', Sinclair wrote of *Pilgrimage*. Sinclair and Richardson were fascinated by the possibility that experience may be primarily, rather than ultimately or absolutely, indivisible and structureless.

The term 'feminine prose' is actually Richardson's: it comes from her introduction to the 1938 edition of *Pilgrimage*:

> Feminine prose, as Charles Dickens and James Joyce have delightfully shown themselves to be aware, should properly be unpunctuated, moving from point to point without formal obstructions. And the author of *Pilgrimage* must confess to an

early habit of ignoring, while writing, the lesser of the stereotyped system of signs, and further when sprinkling in what appeared to be necessary, to a small unconscious departure from current usage.[34]

But, as has been indicated, Richardson was not alone in her beliefs: she was drawing on the work of many other women writers who, seeing language as inherently oppressive and male-centred, aimed to challenge it, and who saw the forms of fiction too as potentially restrictive and gender-bound. The work of Sinclair, Richardson and Gertrude Stein thus offers a particularly rich field for the study of the relations between gender, language and literary form: these women writers were by 1920 embarked on many of the projects which, after a lapse of nearly half a century, French feminist theory has recently republicised and redefined. In drawing attention to the arbitrary nature of language, Sinclair, Richardson and Stein identified what was to form the linchpin of linguistic structuralist theory; they wanted too to push against the antithetical nature of language and experience and to stress the seamless and undifferentiated nature of immediate experience (compare Julia Kristeva's notion of the pre-Oedipal, feminine, semiotic *chora*, as opposed to the over-differentiated and over-mediated language/experience of men).

Why did KM, and Virginia Woolf, find these projects distasteful, or simply wrong? Showalter argues that Virginia Woolf's 'flight into androgyny' was caused by a damaging inhibition of feelings of rage and frustration; she also offers a possible clue to KM's rejection of 'feminine prose' in noting the 'punitive' nature of her fiction.[35] Showalter is right about this punitive aspect of KM's art: in it, women who behave rather like KM herself are severely punished for their presumption in questioning conventional sexual roles. For example, the 'fast' and sexually ambiguous Mrs Kember of 'At the Bay' is punished by complete social ostracism and the faithlessness of her handsome husband. It is thus possible to liken KM's rejection of 'feminine prose' to that of Woolf, suggesting that KM too saw in feminine prose possibilities of exposure and subsequent retributive attack, rather than freedom. We might read KM's strictures on the undifferentiated worlds/words of Richardson and Sinclair as over-reaction against something recognised and repressed in herself.

If we look at it in this light, the imagery KM uses in her reviews of Richardson and Sinclair is, to say the least, disconcerting: consider again, for example, that passage in the review of *The Tunnel* in which she describes the operations of a powerful, institutionalised, male memory, which has the power to judge what shall be allowed to 'shine' in the light of consciousness and what shall be consigned to unconsciousness and oblivion: 'And then it is, in the silence, that Memory mounts his throne and judges all that is in our minds – appointing each his separate place, high or low. . . .'[36] KM here seems to privilege male authority, and clarity, over feminine 'confusion' (compare also her *Night and Day* review, in which she comments acidly on Woolf's description of the 'confusion' of the 'finest prose').

There is a great deal of evidence from KM's early writings of her awareness of feminist issues, though it is also true that her response to these issues remained ambiguous. For example, an early notebook entry commenting enthusiastically on a novel by the feminist Elizabeth Robins is offset by an unpublished sketch in which KM dismisses feminists in a tone of quite awesome sentimentality:

> I longed to take them [the feminists] home and show them my babies and make their hair soft and fluffy, and put them in teagowns and then cuddle them – I think they would never go back to their Physical Culture, or the Society for the Promotion of women's Rights.[37]

An ambivalent attitude towards the opportunities afforded by feminism persisted throughout KM's life: like many of the characters in her fiction, she seems to have been torn between a desire to reject the conventional feminine role and a desire to accept it – to annihilate herself, as it were, by identifying completely with it. This ambivalence is clearly related to KM's bisexuality, itself a complex of forces and orientations which biography can only struggle to recover.[38] What is important for her writing is that this sexual ambivalence produced a fiction which is stronger, in feminist terms, than that of Virginia Woolf, who was of course shocked (and frightened?) by KM's exposure of the emptiness behind stereotypical female role-playing in the story 'Bliss'.[39]

I would suggest that KM's fiction is strong in feminist terms because her estrangement from, yet identification with, the feminine enabled her to see it as something learnt, not something given; something chosen, not necessarily determined by biological or psychological fact. In this context, I think it is thus reasonable to see KM's rejection of feminine prose as more than the self-protective strategy which Showalter describes: KM rejected the cultivation of 'the feminine', by such writers as Richardson, as something exclusive, inalienable and necessarily 'other' because this seemed to her untrue to the slippery and ambivalent nature of human sexual identity.

It is important too to see the wider context in which the movement towards 'feminine prose' can itself be seen as the product of particular cultural and historical forces, as can the sympathetic acceptance of its aims by recent French feminist critics such as Julia Kristeva and Hélène Cixous. As critics we are still emerging from the shadow of Jacques Lacan's theory of the 'Oedipal' moment of entry into the symbolic order of language, by means of which the feminine is necessarily defined in terms of lack. It is only comparatively recently that attempts have been made to theorise a positive rather than a negative entry into language for women. Feminist critics[40] are now drawing attention to the work of psychologists who have insisted that, *pace* Lacan, the entry into language is established prior to and independently of the Oedipal moment of repression. It may be, then, that we should now view Lacanian theory as a reflection *of* rather than a reflection *on* phallocratic values; his extraordinarily influential theory of language as by its nature patriarchal may perhaps itself be seen as symptomatic. If this is so, feminist criticism will have to focus again on questions of power, strength and authority in women's writing: this in turn may offer some vindication of the ways in which Katherine Mansfield held on firmly, in theoretical terms, to her own complex position of author-ity in language.

1 The World of Two: Katherine Mansfield and J. M. Murry, 1911–19

I RHYTHM

Katherine Mansfield first met John Middleton Murry in December 1911. In April 1912 she became assistant editor of *Rhythm*, a quarterly magazine of the arts founded by Murry and Michael Sadleir, which had first appeared in June 1911. Murry and KM wrote the following two articles jointly for *Rhythm*. Both for Murry as critic and for KM as creative artist, these articles represent a first positive manifesto (KM had satirised writers such as Bennett and Wells for the *New Age* magazine, but had not suggested any new alternative method or stance for the artist). Murry was very much influenced at this time by the philosophy of Henri Bergson (1859–1941), and, starting from Bergson's initial descriptions of the artist as possessing pre-eminently the power of intuition, developed a romantic idea of the artist as a 'seeker', forging ahead of ordinary men – the artist's vision is thus 'a moment's lifting of the veil' ('Art and Philosophy', *Rhythm*, no. 1). This romantic view of the artist was substantially that of KM, though her idealism was later qualified by a sharp, ironic wit which seems to have been quite out of Murry's range. 'The Meaning of Rhythm' (*Rhythm*, no. 5) and 'Seriousness in Art' (*Rhythm*, no. 6) have a youthful fervour as if KM in particular has been momentarily caught off guard. It is fairly clear that, while the phrasing of the metaphysic of these essays comes largely from Murry, the imagery is KM's.

'The Meaning of Rhythm'

The History of Art has been the history of a misunderstanding of a minority by a majority. The standing confession of this inability to comprehend is the word 'inspiration'. Men have been forced to realize that the work of art is alien to them, and they have attempted to justify the limitations of their vision by denying the artist his own.

'Inspiration' is the eternal protest of democracy against aristocracy. It paralyses the effort to comprehend and the effort to create. It is of all words the most unreal, for it denies the ultimate supremacy of personality. It asserts that the triumph of individuality is a gift and not a conquest. The artist, the leader, wins his victories for himself and alone.

Like inspiration, intuition, a finer and a truer word, has fallen into the hands of the mob. It is used to cloak every form of ignorance and imbecility. It has become a synonym for the hallucination of religious mania, the anticipations of pregnant women, and the cocksure dogmas of intellectual incompetence. Intuition is a purely aristocratic quality. It is the power of divining individuality in other persons and other things. This divination brings with it a boundless admiration for the individuality divined. This admiration is never the admiration born of poverty but of riches. It is absolutely generous, as freedom is generous. It is the wealthier by its own lavishness. It is the utter understanding of one perfect individual by another, and only by this understanding and this generosity does the artist create, for in this admiration alone does he realize himself. He recognizes his own absolute freedom in divining the freedom of others. He has found reality, for we measure the reality of things by measuring their freedom. Freedom, reality, and individuality are three names for the ultimate essence of life. They are the three qualities of the artist. They are the three qualities of this work of art.

Freedom in the artist is a consciousness of superiority. It is a security born of the conviction that he is creative. He has a certainty of knowledge that he sees the reality of things, which frees him for everything. He knows his own power and is without fear or care. He is so secure that he can give himself wholly up to the delight of living. At every moment he finds some newness of life. He is intimate and at one with all that he meets. He is in love with life. He has all the careless self-surrender of the lover. He has all his careless self-assertion. The more absolute his conscious surrender to life, the more powerful and intimate his impulse towards self-assertion. This conscious surrender to life means for the artist the surrender to freedom, reality and individuality, it is these three qualities in himself which he gives to them and takes back again a thousand times stronger, a thousand times more purified for this surrender. For the life of the artist is one long princely giving and princely taking back again that which is his by right of giving. The only true creation comes from the overflow of his riches.

Freedom in the work of art is the expression of the essentials. It demands the immediate rejection of all that does not help to make the expression the adequate symbol of the idea. It protests against the incursion of machine-made realism into modern literature. In its attempt to reproduce art democracy has succeeded in producing journalism. The journalist himself is the arch-democrat, for he denies his own individuality. In his work facts triumph over truth. He is the prince of democrats because for him all things have equal values, that is, no value at all. The journalist himself cannot even dream of freedom, for he is the slave of the unreality of his own making. The artist frees himself by the realities he creates.

Reality in the work of art demands true intuition in the artist. It demands that the artist shall have seen the ultimate through the externals; it is an inevitable and infallible directness of vision. It is not selection, for there are not a thousand things from which the artist may select, there is always only one, the one fact among a million which is true and therefore the artist's own and part of his personality.

Individuality in the work of art is the creation of reality by freedom. It is the triumphant weapon of aristocracy. It is that daring and splendid thing which the mob hates because it cannot understand and by which it is finally subdued. Only by realizing the unity and the strength of the individual in the work of art is the mob brought to the knowledge of its own infinite weakness, and it loathes and is terrified by it.

Art and the artist are perfectly at one. Art is free; the artist is free. Art is real; the artist is real. Art is individual; the artist is individual. Their unity is ultimate and unassailable. It is the essential movement of Life. It is the splendid adventure, the eternal quest for rhythm.

JOHN MIDDLETON MURRY and
KATHERINE MANSFIELD

'Seriousness in Art'

To-day the craft of letters in England is become a trade instead of an art. It is in vain that we seek for any evidence of artistic seriousness in the gigantic output of modern English literature. It is impossible to deny that the majority of our writers are intensely serious in their effort to reach a comfortable competence. They are serious as any tradesman is serious. This attitude of mind is to them their principal commercial asset. Literature for them is at best a somewhat disreputable means to a purely commercial end, means only to be justified by ultimate financial success. For the English public a writer becomes serious when he becomes 'a gentleman', organized and respectable. 'Seriousness' supervenes on the death of adventure. The man whose personality is sunk in a refined home, a baby in a white perambulator and a plate-chest, has attained to 'seriousness'. He has taken the mob seriously. He has adopted their trade-marks. He will give quiet little champagne dinners, and be accounted the equal of the most villainous South African financier. He is serious and successful, having cornered Prostitution, or Adolescence, or Murders on Moors where his new friends merely dealt in Kaffirs.

Certainly the labourer is worthy of his hire; but in art the hire is never the end of the labour. Artistic seriousness is concerned with the labour and not with the hire. Without it the artist can achieve nothing; for it is just the appreciation of this seriousness that makes him artist. It is the profound enthusiasm of the artist for his art. It is the essential distinction between creativeness and mere production, between art and journalism. Art is a perpetual striving towards an ever more adequate symbolic expression of the living realities of the world. It is by virtue of his seriousness that the artist works towards deepening his understanding of these realities and perfecting his expression. Thus seriousness is a conviction of values. At every moment of creation the artist is convinced of one supreme reality which he endeavours to express with the utmost of his power. By virtue of this capacity for utmost endeavour the mould of each successive idea which the artist seeks to express grows more all-embracing, and thus more perfect. Thus seriousness is the very rock on which the supreme creations of art are builded.

For the bagmen of letters, the book financiers, 'seriousness' has a purely external value. They put it on with their evening dress. In this word are summed up all those social virtues so painfully acquired, all those exercises of discipline and self denial whereby the mob regiments its own personality into impotence. It is absolute conformity to the democratic ideal of monotonous millions of mean and petty men. The life of democracy depends upon the absence of enthusiasm and true seriousness. For these two qualities wedded together are the hall-mark of aristocracy, the essentials of the leader. The 'seriousness' of the tradesman is mechanical and based on monotone. True seriousness is a thing alive and spontaneous, liberating the artist for his art, and consciously expanding into ever wider rhythms. It demands an ever wider sweep for its experience and sees therein profounder and profounder meanings, whereas the false seriousness denies the newness of life and finds safety in every limitation imposed upon its experience. True seriousness is an assertion, a courageous acceptance of the unexplored; the false is a negation, a cowardly clinging to the outworn known. The mob treads over this patch of threadbare ground with mechanical regularity, so poverty-stricken in itself that it asks for nothing but the tokens of poverty and is only comfortable and at ease when it finds nothing further. The land whereon these people live is barren and desolate, lying parcelled and monotonous in the midst of an unknown sea. The artists sail in stately golden ships over this familiar and adventurous ocean. Their gay flags of greeting stream in the sunlight; and far-off winds blow in their great sails and in their hair, as they go sailing by. The tiny land folk call to them and beckon them to shore; but the artists see the land that it is barren and miserable, and they sail onwards. Then the little people are frightened, and cry out to them in rage, and abuse them. Their voices are drowned in the mighty swishing of the green waves. But clean and true rings back their answer, the singing of the sailors, the joyful laughter of serene delight.

J. MIDDLETON MURRY and
KATHERINE MANSFIELD

II EXTRACTS FROM LETTERS AND JOURNALS

The years 1911–19 were ones of by now much documented strain and adventure for KM and Murry. They moved restlessly from 'home' to 'home' in England and France; it was also during this period that they became entangled with the Lawrences and first skirmished with Virginia Woolf. Yet despite their involvement with such famous names, they were in a real sense members of what Virginia Woolf cruelly termed 'the underworld': they were outsiders on the literary–social scene. Murry felt excluded from certain circles because of his lower-middle-class English background; KM felt handicapped by her status as a 'little Colonial'. So during this period, although KM was reading widely and working intensively on her own stories, there was no real consolidation of her critical point of view – this came later. The extracts which follow offer a partial 'spiritual autobiography', as Murry might say, for these years of apprenticeship.

Journal, May 1915

THE 'LIFE' OF LIFE

I bought a book by Henry James[1] yesterday and read it, as they say, 'until far into the night'. It was not very interesting or very good, but I can wade through pages and pages of dull, turgid James for the sake of that sudden sweet shock, that violent throb of delight that he gives me at times. I don't doubt this is genius: only there is an extraordinary amount of pan and an amazing *raffiné* flash –

To J. M. Murry, 9 December 1915

I think the *Oxford Book of English Verse*[2] is *very* poor. I read it for hours this morning in bed. I turned over pages and pages and pages. But except for Shakespeare and Marvell and just a handful of others it seems to be a mass of falsity. Musically speaking, hardly anyone seems to *even understand* what the middle of the note is – what that sound is like. It's not perhaps that they are even 'sharp' or 'flat' – it's something much more subtle – they are not playing on the *very note itself.* But when, in despair, I took up the French Book I nearly sautéd from the fenêtre with rage. It's like an endless gallery of French salon furniture sicklied o'er with bed canopies, candelabra, and porcelain cupids, all bow and bottom. Of course, there *are* exceptions.

Journal, 1916

Having read the whole of *The Idiot* through again, and fairly carefully, I feel slightly more bewildered than I did before as regards Nastasya Filippovna's character. She is really not well done. She is badly done. And there grows up as one reads on a kind of irritation, a *balked* fascination, which almost succeeds finally in blotting out those first and really marvellous 'impressions' of her. What was Dostoevsky really aiming at?

'THE POSSESSED.' SHATOV AND HIS WIFE

There is something awfully significant about the attitude of Shatov to his wife, and it is amazing how, when Dostoevsky at last turns a soft but penetrating and full light upon him, how we have managed to gather a great deal of knowledge of his character from the former vague side-lights and shadowy impressions. He is just what we thought him; he behaves just as we would expect him to do. There is all that crudity and what you might call 'shock-headedness' in his nature – and it is wonderfully tragic that he who is so soon to be destroyed himself should suddenly realise – and through a third person – through a little squealing baby – the miracle just being alive is. . . .

Page 545. ' "Surely you must see that I am in the agonies of childbirth," she said, sitting up and gazing at him with a terrible, hysterical vindictiveness that distorted her whole face. "I curse him before he is born, this child!" '

This vindictiveness is *profoundly* true.

How did Dostoevsky know about that extraordinary vindictive feeling, that relish for little laughter – that comes over women in pain? It is a very secret thing, but it's profound, profound. They don't want to spare the one whom they love. If that one loves them with a kind of blind devotion as Shatov did Marie, they long to torment him, and this tormenting gives them real positive relief. Does this resemble in any way the tormenting that one observes so often in his affairs of passion? Are his women ever happy when they torment their lovers? No, they too are in the agony of labour. They are giving birth to their new selves. And they never believe in their deliverance.

To J. M. Murry, 1917

I got up at that moment to re-read your article on Léon Bloy.[3] The memory of it suddenly *rose* in my mind like a scent. I don't like it. I don't see its use at all, even artistically. It's a *Signature*[4] style of writing and its *appeal* is in some obscure way – to me – mind me: I suppose only to me – indecent. I feel that you are going to uncover yourself and quiver. Sometimes when you write you seem to abase yourself like Dostoevsky did. It's *perfectly* natural to you, I know, but oh, my God, don't do it. It's just the same when you say, talking to Fergusson[5] and me: 'If I am not killed – if *they don't kill* me.' I always laugh at you then because I am ashamed that you should speak so.

What is it? Is it your desire to torture yourself or to pity yourself or something far subtler? I only know that it's tremendously important because it's your way of damnation.

I feel (forgive fanciful me!) that when certain winds blow across your soul they bring the smell from that dark pit and the uneasy sound from those hollow caverns, and you long to lean over the dark swinging danger and just not fall in – but letting us all see meanwhile how low you lean.

Even your style of writing changes then – little short sentences – a hand lifted above the waves – the toss of a curly head above the swirling tumble. It's a terrible thing to be alone. Yes, it is – it is. But don't lower your mask until you have another mask prepared beneath – as terrible as you like – but a mask.

Journal, May 1917

E. M. FORSTER[6]

Putting my weakest books to the wall last night I came across a copy of *Howard's End* and had a look into it. But it's not good enough. E. M. Forster never gets any further than warming the teapot. He's a rare fine hand at that. Feel this teapot. Is it not beautifully warm? Yes, but there ain't going to be no tea.

And I can never be perfectly certain whether Helen was got with child by Leonard Bast or by his fatal forgotten umbrella. All things considered, I think it must have been the umbrella.

Journal, 1917

Tchehov makes me feel that this longing to write stories of such uneven length is quite justified. 'Geneva' is a long story, and 'Hamilton'[7] is very short, and this ought to be written to my brother really, and another about the life in New Zealand. Then there is Bavaria. 'Ich liebe Dich, Ich liebe Dich', floating out on the air ... and then there is Paris. God! When shall I write all these things and how?

Is that all? Can that be all? That is not what I meant at all.[8]

To Dorothy Brett,[9] 11 October 1917

It seems to me so extraordinarily right that you should be painting Still Lives just now. What can one do, faced with this wonderful tumble of round bright fruits, but gather them and play with them – and *become them*, as it were. When I pass the apple stalls I cannot help stopping and staring until I feel that I, myself, am changing into an apple, too – and that at any moment I may produce an apple, miraculously, out of my own being like the conjuror produces the egg. When you paint apples do you feel that your breasts and your knees become apples, too? Or do you think this the greatest nonsense. I don't. I am *sure* it is not. When I write about ducks I swear that I am a white duck with a round eye, floating in a pond fringed with yellow blobs and taking an occasional dart at the other duck with the round eye, which floats upside down beneath me. In fact this whole process of becoming the duck (what Lawrence would, perhaps, call this 'consummation with the duck or the apple'[10]) is so thrilling that I can hardly breathe, only to think about it. For although that is as far as most people can get, it is really only the 'prelude'. There follows the moment when you are *more* duck, *more* apple or *more* Natasha than any of these objects could ever possibly be, and so you *create* them anew. . . .

Forgive me. But that is why I believe in technique, too (you asked me if I did.) I do, just because I don't see how art is going to make that divine *spring* into the bounding outlines of things if it hasn't passed through the process of trying to *become* these things before recreating them.

To J. M. Murry, 3 February 1918

I've two 'kick offs' in the writing game. *One* is joy – real joy – the thing that made me write when we lived at Pauline, and that sort of writing I could only do in just that state of being in some perfectly blissful way *at peace*. Then something delicate and lovely seems to open before my eyes, like a flower without thought of a frost or a cold breath – knowing that all about it is warm and tender and 'ready'. And *that* I try, ever so humbly, to express.

The other 'kick off' is my old original one, and (had I not known love) it would have been my all. Not hate or destruction (both are beneath contempt as real motives) but an *extremely* deep sense of hopelessness, of everything doomed to disaster, almost wilfully, stupidly, like the almond tree and 'pas de nougat pour le noël'. There! as I took out a cigarette paper I got it exactly – a *cry against corruption* – that is *absolutely* the nail on the head. Not a protest – a *cry*, and I mean corruption in the widest sense of the word, of course.

To J. M. Murry, 27 February 1918

I have read *Le P'tit*.[11] It's *very* good – very well done. I think it's got one fault, or perhaps I am too ready to be offended by this. I think the physical part of Le P'tit's feeling for Lama is unnecessarily accentuated. I think if I'd written it I wouldn't have put it in at all – not on his side. On hers, yes. But never once on his. Am I wrong, do you think? Yes, of course, I agree it's well done, that part, but I would have left it more mysterious. Lama must do all she does, and Le P'tit must say: 'Si tu savais comme je t'aime!' But 'lorsqu'un spontané baiser dans l'affolement furieuse de l'instinct chez le jeune homme ...' that I don't like. . . .

But I do find the French language, style, attack, point of view, hard to stomach at present. It's all *tainted*. It all seems to me to lead to dishonesty – Dishonesty Made Easy – made superbly easy. All these *half* words – these words which have never really been born and seen the light – like 'me trouble' – 'tiède' – 'blottant' – 'inexprimable' (these are bad examples, but you know the kinds I mean and the phrases and whole paragraphs that go with them) – they won't at the last moment, *do* at all. Some of them are charming and one is loth to do without them, but they are like certain plants – once they are in your garden they spread and spread and spread, and make a show perhaps, but they are *weeds*. No, I get up hungry from the French language. I have too great an appetite for the real thing to be put off with pretty little kickshaws, and I am offended intellectually that 'ces gens' think they can so take me in.

It's the result of Shakespeare, I think. The English language is damned difficult, but it's also damned rich, and so clear and bright that you can search out the darkest places with it. Also it's *heavenly* simple and true. Do you remember where Paulina says:

> I, an old turtle,
> Will wing me to some withered bough,[12]
> And there my mate that's never to be found again
> Lament till I am lost.

You can't beat that. I *adore* the English language, and that's a fact.

> Your eyes be musical, your dewy feet
> Have freshly trod the lawns for timeless hours,
> O young and lovely dead!

There's a man who can 'use' it!
That is all very badly put. But do you agree?

To J. M. Murry, 26 May 1918

Although, like all poor Gissing's books,[13] it's written with cold wet feet under a wet umbrella, I do feel that if his feet had been dry and the umbrella furled, it would have been extremely good. As it is, the woman of the book is quite a little creation. The whole is badly put together, and there is so much which is entirely irrelevant. He's very clumsy, very stiff, and alas, poor wretch! almost all his 'richness' is eaten up by fogs, catarrh, Gower Street, landladies with a suspicious eye, wet doorsteps, Euston Station.

To J. M. Murry, 5 June 1918

Last night (this letter is like kalter Aufschnitt, please forgive it) I read *The Well-Beloved* by Thomas Hardy. It really is *appallingly bad, simply rotten* – withered, bony and pretentious. This is very distressing. I thought it was going to be such a find and hugged it home from the library as though I were a girl of fifteen. Of course, I wouldn't say this about it to another human being except you – c'est entendu. The style is so PREPOSTEROUS, too. I've noticed that before in Hardy occasionally – a pretentious, snobbish, schoolmaster vein (Lawrence echoes it), an 'all about Berkeley Square-ishness', too. And then to think, as he does, that it is the study of a temperament! I hope to God he's ashamed of it now at any rate. You won't like me writing like this about him. But don't you know the feeling? If a man is 'wonderful' you want to fling up your arms and cry 'Oh, do *go on* being wonderful. Don't be less wonderful.' (Which is unreasonable, of course.)

Journal, August 1918

THE MIDDLE OF THE NOTE[14]

Whenever I have a conversation about Art which is more or less interesting I begin to wish to God I could destroy all that I have written and start again: it all seems like so many 'false starts'. Musically speaking, it is not – has not been – in the middle of the note – you know what I mean? When, on a cold morning perhaps, you've been playing and it has sounded all right – until suddenly, you *realise* you are warm – you have only just begun to play.

The following extract from a letter to Ottoline Morrell, though not strictly about literary matters, is crucial for an understanding of KM's attitude to the war. Like Lawrence, she tried initially to retreat before the horror of the war, but, impelled by grief over the death of her brother in its early stages, went on to seek a deeper understanding of 'the meaning of it all'. Her feeling that no writer could afford to ignore the social and metaphysical implications of the war became a major theme in her *Athenaeum* criticism.

To Ottoline Morrell,[15] *November 1918*

These preparations for Festivity[16] are too odious. In addition to my money complex I have a food complex. When I read of the preparations that are being made in all the workhouses throughout the land – when I think of all those toothless old jaws guzzling for the day – and then of all that beautiful youth feeding the fields of France – Life is almost too ignoble to be borne. Truly one must hate humankind in the mass, hate them as passionately as one loves the few, the very few. Ticklers, squirts, portraits 8 times as large as life of Lloyd George and Beatty blazing across the sky – and drunkenness and brawling and destruction. I keep seeing all these horrors, bathing in them again and again (God knows I don't want to) and then my mind fills with the wretched little picture I have of my brother's grave. What is the meaning of it all?

2 'Wanted, a New World': the *Athenaeum*, 1919–20

Murry was offered the editorship of the *Athenaeum*[1] in January 1919, and from April 1919 until December 1920 KM reviewed novels weekly for the paper. She took her job as a reviewer very seriously, and indeed reviewing seems to have taken over from fiction writing during this period of her life. She and Murry were intensely aware that in the *Athenaeum* they had the literary platform they had longed for, and they determined to *use* the opportunity offered them: they felt it was their duty, as it had been long ago in the 'palmy' *Rhythm* days, to stand up for 'seriousness in art', as opposed to the superficial 'pastime' art and literature which seemed acceptable to many. In this respect, KM's critical stance can be read as having an ethical as well as an aesthetic dimension: the two were for her interdependent. Throughout her reviews, too, she stressed the relationship between – though not the identity of – 'art and life',[2] writing, for example, in a review of *Esther Waters*,

> And yet we would say without hesitation that *Esther Waters* is not a great novel, and never could be a great novel, because it has not, from first to last, the faintest stirring of the breath of life. It is dry as the remainder biscuit after a voyage.[3]

Hence the special quality of her criticism, which, like her work, cuts across the neat categories we have developed to classify early-twentieth-century literature. KM is a romantic experimentalist in prose, having affinities with D. H. Lawrence on the one hand and Virginia Woolf on the other. Her criticism is on the whole more like that of Lawrence than that of Woolf, and in this sense the grouping of KM, Murry and Lawrence around *Rhythm* (Lawrence became a contributor in 1913) seems in retrospect not entirely arbitrary – the three represent a distinctive 'romantic' tendency within the modernist literary movement.

Though KM wrote little fiction during this period, her journal and letters are marked by an access of confidence at about the time Murry took over the *Athenaeum*. She has a new poise and authority: this may be related to Murry's rise from the 'underworld' to his position as influential editor. More importantly, her fiction gains immeasurably in strength in that period immediately following on from the reviewing-stint, and it seems reasonable to suggest that the clarification of certain precepts in her *Athenaeum* criticism contributed to the sureness of tone in the fiction from this period on.

I   EXTRACTS FROM LETTERS AND JOURNALS[4]

To Virginia Woolf, May 1919

Tchehov has a very interesting letter published in next week's A ...[5] What the writer does is not so much to *solve* the question but to *put* the question. There must be the question put. That seems to me a very nice dividing line between the true and the false writer.

KM here 'crystallises' (to borrow a critical term used by Murry and herself) Chekhov's thought. The relevant passage from Chekhov's letters runs as follows:

> It seems to me that it is not the business of novelists to solve questions such as – God, pessimism, and so forth. The business of the novelist is merely to describe how and under what circumstances his people spoke or thought of God, or pessimism. An artist must not be a judge of his people or of what they say, but only an impartial witness.   (*Athenaeum*, 18 April 1919)

To J. M. Murry, 25 November, 1919

I don't think SW[6] brought it off with George Eliot. He never gets under way. The cart wheels want oiling. I think, too, he is ungenerous. She was a deal more than that. Her English warm ruddy quality is hardly mentioned. She *was* big, even though she was 'heavy' too. But think of some of her pictures of country life – the breadth, the sense of sun lying on warm barns, great warm kitchens at twilight when the men came home from the fields, the feeling of *beasts*, horses and cows, the peculiar passion she has for horses. (When Maggie Tulliver's lover walks with her up and down the lane and asks her to marry, he leads his great red horse, and the beast is foaming – it has been hard ridden and there are dark streaks of sweat on its flanks – the *beast is the man*, one feels *she* feels in some queer inarticulate way.) . . .

The Duhamel[7] is, of course, another eye-opener. The idea that they should surrender something of their personality ... that started a terrific excitement bubbling in me. It's true of all artists, isn't it? It gives me another *critical point of view* about an artist and quite a new one. I mean – to find out what the man is subduing, to mark that side of him being gradually absorbed (even as it were without his knowing it) into the side of him he has chosen to explore, strengthening it, reinforcing it even while *he thinks* it is subdued away.

To J. M. Murry, 5 December 1919

Now about your talk at Delamare's[8] on poetry. No, you're NOT too serious. I think you are a trifle over-anxious to assure people how serious you are. You antagonize them sometimes or set them doubting because of your emphasis on your sincerity. In reviewing again you cry sometimes, in your sincerity: these are the things which have been done, which have happened, to *me* or to *us*. I think as a critic that *me* or *us* is superfluous. If they must be there, then you must write a poem or a story. People are not *simple* enough – Life is not simple enough – to bear it otherwise. It fills me with a queer kind of shame; one hears oneself whispering in one's soul to you: 'Cover yourself – cover yourself quickly. Don't let them see!' That they think you are asking for alms, for pity, doesn't matter. That, of course, is just their corruption – their falsity. Nevertheless, though they are wrong, I do not think you are right. If you speak for your generation, *speak*, but don't say 'I speak for my generation', for the force is then gone from your cry. When you know you are a voice crying in the wilderness, *cry*, but don't say 'I am a voice crying in the wilderness.' To my thinking (and I am as you know so infinitely, incomparably nearer the public than you) the force of either the blow you strike or the praise you want to sing is *broken* by this – what is it? Is it the most infernal modesty? Innocence?

To J. M. Murry, 8 December 1919

Nevertheless, it seems to me that the false world has wounded you – has changed your 'word' from what it should be to what it is. You ought not to have to say these things.[9] It is wrong that they should have been forced from you. You see, I don't believe that the war has done these things to you: I don't believe you are maimed for life – that you *go on* certainly, but that you never can recover. (Your generation I mean that you speak for) I think these are the conclusions arrived at by thinking: granted such a war, granted such a *reception* of such a war, granted such falsity, indifference, squalor and callousness – their effect upon an intellect would be so and so ... But this intellectual reasoning is never *the whole truth*. It's not *the artist's truth* – not *creative*. If man were an intellect it would do, but man ISN'T. Now I must be fair, I must be fair. Who am I to be certain that I understand? There's always Karori to shout after me. *Shout* it. I've re-read 'The Question' and 'The Republic of the Spirit'. 'The Question' is very brilliant. But it's an *étude* – isn't it? *Tour de force sur les écharpes*? Isn't it? The other is the best essay in the book. I think it might have been written by a famous MONK. As I read, I felt: Yes, yes, yes, but now let me turn and kiss somebody and let there be music ...

Now I do not want you to think it's the female in me that wants to kiss somebody after these essays. It is not because I am incapable of detachment that they seem to me *un*-warm (in the sense that fertility is warm. I keep seeing a golden hen on her eggs). For you are not detached. If you were detached, you would not have been influenced in the same way by the spirit of the times. Yet it is not the *complete you* who is influenced: it is the intellectual you. The *complete you* rebels against the intellectual you at times and wrestles and overthrows it. Which wins out, after the book if finished, in the mind of the reader?

p. 19 'We are maimed and broken for ever. Let us not deceive ourselves.'

p. 86 'Tchehov's sense of the *hopeless indescribable* beauty of the *infinitely weary* pattern.'

p. 97 'And even that to such contemplation our own *utter* discomfiture is beautiful.'

p. 110 'Yet we feel that the effort to respond to the *Sursum Corda* will be as long and may be more terrible still.'

p. 110 'A part, how great we do not know, of our soul is become *for ever* numbed and insentient. But with what remains we feel, and we feel no joy.'

p. 117 'And while we reach back *timidly* into the past to discover the sequence of our wounds.'

p. 131 'We are afraid to speak of it because we know in our hearts that the breath of the very word will find us *naked* and *shivering* ...'

p. 156 'The possibility which we had desired stood before us in the *frozen intolerable* rigidity of a law. Against it we might dash our minds but they would break.

p. 166 'The impulse is almost overwhelming to withdraw into ourselves and discover in the *endurance* of our souls ...'

p. 216 'In a life in which the gold has dimmed to grey.'

p. 218 'A menacing instinct warns us that we are somehow maimed.'

I have just copied these few things because though I know it is not all 'like that' they are there – and they are important. They DO give the tone. You know, Bogey, they seem to me deathly. They frighten me. I don't believe them – but that's beside the question. What I feel is that they cannot be the VITAL you? Were the world not what it is, that you would not be alive today. Whatever the world were, the you of certain of your poems – of parts of *Cinnamon and Angelica* – will always be there. It seems to me that the intellect only ceases to be a devil when the soul is *supreme* and *free*.

To J. M. Murry, 13 December 1919

GBS on Butler is very fine indeed.[10] He has such a grip of his subject. I admire his tenacity as a reviewer and the way in which his mind follows Butler with a steady light – does not waver over him, find him, lose him, travel over him. At the same time it's queer he should be (GBS) so uninspired. There is not the faintest hint of inspiration in that man. This chills me. You know the feeling that a great writer gives you: 'My spirit has been fed and refreshed: it has partaken of something new.' One could not possibly feel that about Shaw. It's the clang of the gate that remains with you when all's over. What it amounts to is that Shaw is anything you like, but he's not an artist. Don't you get when you read his plays a sense of extraordinary *flatness*? They may be extremely amusing at moments, but you are always laughing *at* and never *with*. Just the same in his prose: You may agree as much as you like, but he is writing *at* not *with*. There's no getting over it: he's a kind of concierge in the house of literature – sits in a glass case, sees everything, knows everything, examines the letters, *cleans the stairs*, but has no part, no part in the life that is going on.

Journal, 29 February 1920

Oh, to be a *writer*, a real writer given up to it and to it alone! Oh, I failed to-day; I turned back, I looked over my shoulder, and immediately it happened, I felt as though I too were struck down.

The day turned cold and dark on the instant. It seemed to belong to summer twilight in London, to the clang of the gates as they close the garden, to the deep light painting the high houses, to the smell of leaves and dust, to the lamp-light, to that stirring of the senses, to the langour of twilight, the breath of it on one's cheek, to all those things which (I feel to-day) are gone from me for ever ... I feel to-day that I shall die soon and suddenly: but not of my lungs.

There are moments when Dickens is possessed by this power of writing: he is carried away. That is bliss. It certainly is not shared by writers to-day. For instance, the death of Cheedle:[11] dawn falling upon the edge of night. One realises exactly the mood of the writer and how he wrote, as it were, for himself, but it was not his will. He *was* the falling dawn, and he *was* the physician going to Bar. And again when ...

Journal, April 1920

THE FLOWERING OF THE SELF

When autograph albums were the fashion – sumptuous volumes bound in soft leather, and pages so delicately tinted that each tender sentiment had its own sunset sky to faint, to die upon – the popularity of that most sly, ambiguous, difficult piece of advice: 'To thine own self be true' was the despair of collectors. How dull it was, how boring, to have the same thing written six times over! And then, even if it was Shakespeare, that didn't prevent it – oh, *l'âge d'innocence*! – from being dreadfully obvious. Of course, it followed as the night the day that if one was true to oneself ... True to oneself! which self? Which of my many – well really, that's what it looks like coming to – hundreds of selves? For what with complexes and repressions and reactions and vibrations and reflections, there are moments when I feel I am nothing but the small clerk of some hotel without a proprietor, who has all his work cut out to enter the names and hand the keys to the wilful guests.

Nevertheless, there are signs that we are intent as never before on trying to puzzle out, to live by, our own particular self. *Der Mensch muss frei sein* – free, disentangled, single. Is it not possible that the rage for confession, autobiography, especially for memories of earliest childhood, is explained by our persistent yet mysterious belief in a self which is continuous and permanent; which, untouched by all we acquire and all we shed, pushes a green spear through the dead leaves and through the mould, thrusts a scaled bud through years of darkness until, one day, the light discovers it and shakes the flower free and – we are alive – we are flowering for our moment upon the earth? This is the moment which, after all, we live for – the moment of direct feeling when we are most ourselves and least personal.[12]

Journal, August 1920

'Then the train rattled among the housetops and among the ragged sides of houses torn down to make way for it, and over the swarming streets and under the fruitful earth ... A little more, and again it roared across the river, a great rocket: spurning the watery turnings and doublings with ineffable contempt, and going straight to its end, as Father Time goes to his. To whom it is no matter what living waters run high or low, reflect the heavenly lights and darknesses, produce their little growth of weeds and flowers, turn here, turn there, are noisy or still, are troubled or at rest, for their course has one sure termination, though their sources and devices are many.

Then a carriage ride succeeded, near the solemn river, stealing away by night, as all things steal away, by night and by day, so quietly yielding to the attraction of the loadstone rock Eternity ... (*Our Mutual Friend.*)

Dickens on Death. It's always the same gesture. What does it imply?

To J. M. Murry, 25 September 1920

I heard again from Methuen today. They now say they'd like 2 books for next spring. I think there must have been some trunk work, some back stair work in this on [your part]. But I'll see what I can do without promising in my fatal way what I can't perform. I wish I could begin real creative work. I haven't yet. It's the atmosphere, the ... tone which is hard to get. And without it nothing is worth doing. I have such a horror of *triviality* ... a great part of my Constable book[13] is *trivial*. It's not good enough. You see it's too late to beat about the bush any longer. They are cutting down the cherry trees; the orchard is sold – that is really the atmosphere I want. Yes, the dancing and the dawn and the Englishman in the train who said 'jump!' – all these, with the background. I feel – this is jet sincere –

that you and I are the only 2 persons who realize this really. That's our likeness and that's what makes us, too, the creatures of our time.

Speaking of something else, which is nevertheless connected – it is an awful temptation, in face of all these novels to cry 'Woe – woe!' I cannot conceive how writers who have lived through our times can *drop* these last ten years and revert to why Edward didn't understand Vi's reluctance to be seduced or (see Bennett) why a dinner of twelve covers needs remodelling. If I did not review novels I'd never read them. The writers (practically all of them) seem to have no idea of what one means by continuity. It is a difficult thing to explain. Take the old Tartar waiter in *Anna* who serves Levin and Stepan – Now, Tolstoy only has to touch him and he gives out a note and this note is somehow important, persists, is a part of the whole book. But all these other men – they introduce their cooks, aunts, strange gentlemen, and so on, and once the pen is off them they are *gone* – dropped down a hole. Can one explain this by what you might call – a *covering* atmosphere – Isn't that a bit too vague? Come down O Youth from yonder Mountain height and give your Worm a staff of reason to assist her. What it *boils down to* is ... 'either the man can make his people live and keep 'em alive or he can't'. But criticks better that.

To J. M. Murry, 13 October 1920

I am amazed at the sudden 'mushroom growth' of cheap psychoanalysis everywhere. *Five* novels one after the other are based on it: it's in everything. And I want to prove it won't do – it's turning Life into a *case*. And yet, of course, I do believe one ought to be able to – not ought – one's novel if it's a good one will be capable of being *proved* scientifically to be correct. Here – the thing that's happening now is – *the impulse to write is a different impulse*. With an artist – one has to allow – Oh tremendously – for the sub-conscious element in his work. He writes he knows not what – he's *possessed*. I don't mean, of course, always, but when he's *inspired* – as a sort of divine flower to all his terrific hard gardening there comes this subconscious ... wisdom. Now these people who are nuts on analysis seem to me to have *no* subconscious at all. They write to *prove* – not to tell the truth.[14]

Journal, 1920

COLERIDGE'S TABLE TALK

'It is intolerable when men, who have no other knowledge, have not even a competent understanding of that world in which they are always living, and to which they refer everything.'

Hear! Hear!

'Although contemporary events obscure past events in a living man's life, yet, so soon as he is dead, and his whole life is a matter of history, one action stands out as conspicuously as another.'

Totally wrong!

'Intense study of the Bible will keep any writer from being *vulgar* in point of style.'

In point of *language*.

'I, for one, do not call the sod under my feet my country. But language, religion, laws, government, blood – identity in these makes men of one country.'

The sod under my feet makes *mine*.

' "Most women have no character at all," said Pope, and meant it for satire. Shakespeare, who knew man and woman much better, saw that it, in fact, was the perfection of woman to be characterless. Everyone wishes a Desdemona or Ophelia for a wife – creatures who, though they may not always understand you, do always feel you and feel with you.'

Now you are being silly.

COLERIDGE'S LECTURES ON SHAKESPEARE

STAGE ILLUSION

'Not only are we never absolutely deluded – or anything like it, but the attempt to cause the highest delusion possible to beings in their senses sitting in a theatre, is a gross fault, incident only to low minds, which, feeling that they cannot affect the heart or head permanently, endeavour to call forth the momentary affections. There ought never to be more pain than is compatible with co-existing pleasure, and to be amply repaid by thought.'

That is superb. Tchehov *v.* Barrie. Think here of *The Cherry Orchard*, where orchard, birds, etc., are quite unnecessary. The whole effect of dawn is produced by *blowing out the candle*.

An author should 'have felt so deeply on certain subjects, or in consequence of certain imaginations, as to make it *almost a necessity of his nature to seek for sympathy* – no doubt, with that honourable desire of permanent action which distinguishes genius.'

'It is to be lamented that we judge of books by books, instead of referring what we read to our own experience.'

'The second ... distinct cause of this diseased disposition of taste [i.e. perceiving strangeness in the language of the poetic drama where we should feel exultation] is ... the security, the comparative equability and *ever-increasing sameness of human life.*'

No! No! No!

'In his very first productions, Shakespeare projected his mind out of his own particular being, and felt, and made others feel, on subjects no way connected with himself, except by force of contemplation and that sublime faculty by which a great mind becomes that on which it meditates.'

Thou hast said it, Coleridge!

'Or again imagination acts by so carrying on the eye of the reader as to make him almost lose the consciousness of words, – to make him see everything flashed, as Wordsworth has grandly and appropriately said, –

> *Flashed* upon that inward eye.
> Which is the bliss of solitude.

And this without exciting any painful or laborious attention, without *any anatomy of description*, (a fault not uncommon in descriptive poetry) – but with the sweetness and easy movement of nature.'

'There are men who can write passages of deepest pathos and even sublimity on circumstances personal to themselves and stimulative of their own passions; but they are not, therefore, on this account poets.'

Oh, Coleridge!

'It is my earnest desire – my passionate endeavour – to enforce at various times and by various arguments and instances the close and reciprocal connexion of just taste with pure morality. Without that acquaintance with the heart of man, or that docility and childlike gladness to be made acquainted with it, which those only can have who dare look at their own hearts – and that with a steadiness which religion only has the power of reconciling with sincere humility; – without this, and the modesty produced by it, I am deeply convinced that no man, however wide his erudition, however patient his antiquarian researches, can possibly understand, or be worthy of understanding the writings of Shakespeare.'

Thou – thou art the man with whom I would speak. Should we mean the same by religion? We should not quarrel. (*October 21, 1920.*)

'Hamlet's wildness is but half false; he plays that subtle trick of pretending to act only when he is very near really being what he acts.'

Profound.

'*Banquo*:

> The earth hath bubbles, as the water has
> And these are of them: – Whither are they vanished?

Macbeth:

> Into the air; and what seemed corporal, melted
> As breath into the wind. – Would they had staid!

Is it too minute to notice the appropriateness of the simile "as breath", etc., in a cold climate?'

No; it's perfect.

COLERIDGE ON HAMLET

'Anything finer than this conception and working out of a great character is merely impossible. Shakespeare wished to impress upon us the truth, that action is the chief end of existence – that no faculties of intellect, however brilliant, can be considered valuable, or indeed otherwise than as misfortunes, if they withdraw us from, or render us repugnant to action, and lead us to think and think of doing, until the time has elapsed when we can do anything effectually. In enforcing this moral truth, Shakespeare has shown the fullness and force of his powers; all that is amiable and excellent in nature is combined in Hamlet, with the exception of one quality. He is a man living in meditation, called upon to act by every motive human and divine, but the great object of his life is defeated by continually resolving to do, yet doing nothing but resolve.'

Who could understand that better than thou, Coleridge? I have no doubt that thou wert accusing thyself ... And yet I wonder whether all great men, however developed their power of action, do not always think thus of themselves. They are ridden by the desire to act, and the performance is only the step to another ... In another sense Fleance always escapes. (Or was that because Macbeth merely employed his murderers?) Be that as it may, Macbeth holds this phrase which has in it every faintest atom of the feelings of a writer: *This restlessness of ecstasy.*

This book [Coleridge's *Essays and Lectures on Shakespeare*] is certainly a great treasure. But I like to 'record' that there is much in it which was suited only to its time. I feel we have advanced very far since the days of Coleridge, and that he (because he is so restrained and handicapped by his *audience*) would have been far more enlightening about Shakespeare to-day.

To J. M. Murry, 30 October 1920

At the same time the whole book seems to me *in*-decent.[15] Perhaps I feel more than anything that she's one of those people who have no past and no future. She's capable of her girlish pranks and follies today – in fact, she's at the mercy of herself now and for ever as she was then. *And that's bad.* We only live by somehow absorbing the past – changing it. I mean really examining it and dividing what is important from what is not (for there IS waste) and transforming it so that it becomes part of the life of the spirit and we are *free of it*. It's no longer our personal past, it's just in the highest possible sense, our servant. I mean that it is no longer our master. That is the wrong image. I used to think this process was fairly unconscious. Now I feel just the contrary. With Mrs A this process (by which the artist and the 'living being' lives) never takes place. She is for ever driven. She is of the school of Ottoline, isn't she?

'I am the Cup that thirsteth for the Wine' –

These half people are very queer – very tragic, really. They are neither simple – nor are they artists. They are between the two and yet they have the desires (no, appetites) of both. I believe their *secret whisper* is: 'If only I had found THE MAN I might have been anything ... .' But the man isn't born and so they turn to life and parade and preen and confess and dare – and lavish themselves on what they call *Life*. 'Come woo me – woo me.' How often I've *seen* that in Ottoline as her restless and distracted glance swept the whole green country-side ...

To Sydney and Violet Schiff,[16] *4 November 1920*

I'm sure I've read 20 novels this autumn by LADY writers that might all be called *How I lost my Virginity!* If that wasn't bad enough – they never tell the truth – they always tell *How I WISHED to lose my Virginity,* and in fact I don't believe they ever did lose it.

I wish there were 6 or 7 writers who wrote for themselves and let the world go hang. But where are they? As to critics – to have to print Herbert Read is enough proof of their scarcity. I can't bear Herbert Read; he always sounds so puffed up and so dull.

To J. M. Murry, 7 November 1920

I sometimes wonder whether the act of surrender[17] is not the greatest of all – the highest. It is one of the [most] difficult of all. Can it be accomplished or even apprehended except by the *aristocrats* of this world? You see it's so immensely complicated. It 'needs' real humility and at the same time an absolute belief in one's own essential freedom. It is an act of faith. At the last moments like all great acts it is *pure risk.* This is true for me as a human being and as a writer. Dear Heaven! how hard it is to let go – to step into the blue. And yet one's creative life depends on it and one *desires* to do nothing else.

To J. M. Murry, 21 November 1920

EB [Edmund Blunden] had Masefield delivered into his hands. It's queer how an author always gives away finally his *secret weakness.* Here is *anatomy of description instead of creative power:*[18] it comes of course from a weakness of creative power. One thinks the effect can be produced by an *infinite piling on.* But there's a whole fascinating argument dropped there. EB evidently wishes to keep in with JM (or perhaps that's unkind of me).

The review of Ruskin, too. Fancy talking of Ruskin's 'marvellous confidence in himself'. Fancy being taken in to that extent. If the reverse was ever true of a man it was of R. His efforts are pitifully obvious to overcome this.

To J. M. Murry, November 1920

And about 'Poison'.[19] I could write about that for pages. But I'll try and condense what I've got to say. The story is told by (evidently) a worldly, rather cynical (not wholly cynical) man *against* himself (but not altogether) when he was so absurdly young. You know how young by his idea of what woman is. She has been up to now, only the *vision*, only she who passes. You realize that? And here he has put *all* his passion into this Beatrice. It's *promiscuous love*, not understood as such by him; perfectly understood as such by her. But you realize the vie de luxe they are living – the very table – sweets, liqueurs, lilies, pearls. And you realize? she expects a letter from someone calling her away? *Fully* expects it? Which accounts for her farewell AND her declaration. And when it doesn't come even her *commonness* peeps out – the newspaper touch of such a woman. She can't disguise her chagrin. She gives herself away … He, of course, laughs at it now, and laughs at her. Take what he says about her 'sense of order' and the crocodile. But he also regrets the self who dead privately would have been young enough to have actually wanted to *marry* such a woman. But I meant it to be light – tossed off – and yet through it – oh, subtly – the lament for youthful belief. These are the rapid confessions one receives sometimes from a glove or a cigarette or a hat.

I suppose I haven't brought it off in 'Poison'. It wanted a light, light hand – and then with that newspaper a sudden … let me see, *lowering* of it all – just what happens in promiscuous love after passion. A glimpse of staleness. And the story is told by the man who gives himself away and hides his traces at the same moment.

I realize it's quite a different kind to 'Miss Brill' or 'The Young Girl' (She's not 'little', Bogey; in fact, I saw her big, slender, like a colt.)

To J. M. Murry, 5 December 1920

The whole paper needs a stricter form – or could do with one, I feel, a more stringent form that is scrupulously adhered to. But I realize the difficulty of this with writers like KM and Co. who never can learn the length of a page. Still they ought to be hauled over the coals. A big nasty cut now and again would larn 'em.

The front par[agraph]s are – not very interesting, are they? They want more diversity – the *par.* one subject. If they run on they might as well be a short article. I think the Science article is valuable. It's a pity it can't be more varied. Where's your medical man – the man who wrote about the fatigued frog? *Orton* ought to be sent a book or two for 1 col. reviews, too.

Marginalia is utterly feeble. It had a moment, a little spurt, a few weeks ago, but ever since then it has been dead as a nib. '100 years ago' is the dust-bin, tho', Boge.

If the paper is shorter, it wants to be more *defined, braced up, tighter.*

In my reckless way I would suggest all reviews were signed and all were put into the first person. I think that would give the whole paper an amazing lift-up. A paper that length must be *definite, personal*, or die. It can't afford the 'we' – 'in our opinion'. To sign reviews, to put them in the 1st person stimulates curiosity, *makes for correspondence*, gives it (to be 19-eleventyish[20]) GUTS. You see it's a case of leaning out of the window with a board and a nail, *or* a bouquet, *or* a flag – administering whichever it is and retiring *sharp*. This seems to me essential. Signed reviews are tonic: the time has gone by for any others. I do wish you could work this. I am sure it would attract the public. And there's rather a 'trop de livres, trop de livres' faint cry in it. I read the first par. of about 4 reviews and I begin to whimper faintly.

You're all right, but the others are not. A letter ought to be drafted to your regular contributors asking them, now that the reviews are to be signed (supposing that were to happen) – asking them to pull themselves together and make their *attack* stronger. Do you know what I mean? I feel inclined to say to them, as if I were taking their photographs: '*Look Fearless'*. They are huddled up.

To J. M. Murry, *December 1920*

Your Hardy[21] doesn't quite come off to my thinking. You seem to be hinting at a special understanding between yourself and the author. That's not fair: it puts me off. You (in the name of your age, true, but not quite, not wholly) intrude your age, your experience of suffering … This destroys the balance.

Your Keats is performance, right enough, but it's more promise. Makes me feel you ought to write a book on Keats. It's deeply interesting. The last paragraph is a pity – when you praise Sir Sidney [Sir Sidney Colvin (Murry's note)]. Here again I seem to catch a faint breath of *pride*.

I think Edward Thomas is seen out of proportion. It's not in his poems; he's not *all that*. Your emotions are too apparent. I feel one ought to replace Thomas with another and say it all about *him*. There was the beginning of all that in Thomas but you've filled it out yourself – to suit what you wanted him to be. It's not wholly sincere, either, for that reason.

Let me make my meaning clearer. Take your Tchekhov. Now you make Tchekhov greater than one sees him but NOT greater than he was. This is an *important dangerous* distinction. A critic must see a man as great as his potentialities but NOT greater. Falsity creeps in immediately then.

You ought to guard against this. Its another 'aspect' of your special pleading danger – as in your essay on Hardy. In your tremendously just desire to prove him a major poet, you mustn't make yourself Counsel for the Prisoner! I mean that in all its implications.

You might have borne this trick of yours in mind when you are so down on STC [Coleridge] for his idolatry. Remember how Shakespeare *was* regarded at that time – the extraordinary ignorance, stupidity and meanness of the point of view. I don't think you take that into account enough. It's too easy to talk of laudanum and soft brainedness. The reason for his *überfluss* is more psychological. (I don't defend STC but I think he and you are both wrong in 'considering' far too specially a 'special' audience). On the other hand you are splendidly just to his amazing *Venus and Adonis* criticism. (I must say that chapter on *V and A* is a gem of the first water).

Ronsard is interesting because you have conveyed the chap's quality so well, tho' I deeply disagree with one of the 'charming' quotations – the complexion one is perfect.

Now, I'll be franker still. There are still traces of what I call your sham personality in this book and they mar it – the personality that expressed itself in the opening paragraphs of your Santayana review in the *Nation.* Can't you see what a *farce* it makes of your preaching the good life? The good life indeed, – rowing about in your little boat with the worm-eaten ship and chaos! Look here! How *can* you! How can you lay up your sweat in a phial for future generations! I don't ask for false courage from anyone but I do think that even if you are shivering it is your duty as an artist and a man *not* to shiver. The devil and the angel in you both fight in that review. I must speak out plainly because your friends flatter you. They are not really taken in by your 'sham personality', but they are too uncertain of themselves not to pretend that they are, and you are deceived by their pretence because you want to be. It is this which mars you and it is for this reason you will not be popular. It's the BAD in you people can't stomach – not the good. But tho' they don't understand it, they sense it as treachery – as something that *is not done*. Don't be proud of your unpopularity, Bogey. It is right you should be unpopular for this.

II   THE *ATHENAEUM* REVIEWS

KM established a style for the *Athenaeum* reviews which was, as Anthony Alpers puts it, 'a sort of female mandarin, or mandarine, most delicately judged for the needs of the moment as its author's husband tried to win new readers without losing *all* of the paper's old ones'.[22] The misgivings KM had about this reviewing style are discussed in the Introduction: whatever her doubts and scruples, her reviews were immediately successful with the paper's readers. By November 1919 Murry was able to report,

> Your novel page, I know, is one of the features most appreciated in the paper, and any interruption of it would do us great harm. To me, you seem to get better and better every time. You are so *sure*, besides being so delicate. It's quite unlike – in a different class to – anything that's being done in the way of reviewing anywhere to-day. What I feel, and what a great many other people feel, is that as long as your novel page is there, there can't be a really bad number of the *Athenaeum*.'[23]

Extracts from the reviews have been gathered under different headings for ease of reference. Under each heading, the order is chronological by date of publication. Where KM's own comments on the reviews are extant, they are printed following them in italics.

EMINENT NOVELISTS

Review of The Tunnel,[24] *by Dorothy Richardson*
(extract from 'Three Women Novelists', 4 April 1919)

Why was it written? The question does not present itself – it is the last question one would ask after reading *The Tunnel*. Miss Richardson has a passion for registering every single thing that happens in the clear, shadowless country of her mind. One cannot imagine her appealing to the reader or planning out her novel; her concern is primarily, and perhaps ultimately, with herself. 'What cannot I do with this mind of mine!' one can fancy her saying. 'What can I not see and remember and express!' There are times when she seems deliberately to set it a task, just for the joy of realizing again how brilliant a machine it is, and we, too, share her admiration for its power of absorbing. Anything that goes into her mind she can summon forth again, and there it is, complete in every detail, with nothing taken away from it – and nothing added. This is a rare and interesting gift, but we should hesitate before saying it was a great one.

The Tunnel is the fourth volume of Miss Richardson's adventures with her soul-sister Miriam Henderson. Like them, it is composed of bits, fragments, flashing glimpses, half scenes and whole scenes, all of them quite distinct and separate, and all of them of equal importance. There is no plot, no beginning, no middle or end. Things just 'happen' one after another with incredible rapidity and at break-neck speed. There is Miss Richardson, holding out her mind, as it were, and there is Life hurling objects into it as fast as she can throw. And at the appointed time Miss Richardson dives into its recesses and reproduces a certain number of these treasures – a pair of button boots, a night in Spring, some cycling knickers, some large, round biscuits – as many as she can pack into a book, in fact. But the pace kills.

There is one who could not live in so tempestuous an environment as her mind – and he is Memory. She has no memory. It is true that Life is sometimes very swift and breathless, but not always. If we are to be truly alive there are large pauses in which we creep away into our caves of contemplation. And then it is, in the silence, that Memory mounts his throne and judges all that is in our minds – appointing each his separate place, high or low, rejecting this, selecting that – putting this one to shine in the light and throwing that one into the darkness.

We do not mean to say that those large, round biscuits might not be in the light, or the night in Spring be in the darkness. Only we feel that until these things are judged and given each its appointed place in the whole scheme, they have no meaning in the world of art.

> *Criticism: Not   good   enough.*
> *Lukewarm,   shallow   forced.   Very*
> *thin,   pocket   muslin   handkerchief*
> *vocabulary!*
> K.M.

Review of The Moon and Sixpence *by W. S. Maugham*
(extracts from 'Inarticulations', 9 May 1919)

Had Mr Maugham confessed to his hero Charles Strickland, a painter of genius, his great desire to present him, to explain him to the public, with all his eccentricities, violences and odious ways included, we imagine the genius would have retorted in his sardonic way: 'Go to hell. Let them look at my pictures or not look at them – damn them. My painting is all there is to me.' This discouraging reply is not without a large grain of truth. Strickland cut himself off from the body of life, clumsily, obstinately, savagely – hacking away, regardless of torn flesh, and quivering nerves, like some old Maori warrior separating himself from a shattered limb with a piece of sharp shell. What proof have we that he suffered? No proof at all. On the contrary, each fresh ugly blow wrung a grin or chuckle from him, but never the slightest sign that he would have had it otherwise if he could.

If we had his pictures before us, or the memory of them in our mind's eye, this his state of mind might be extremely illuminating, but without them, with nothing to reinforce our knowledge of him but a description of two or three which might apply equally well to a very large number of modern works, we are left strangely unsatisfied. The more so in that Mr Maugham takes extraordinary pains in explaining to us that Strickland is no imaginary character. His paintings are known everywhere, everywhere acclaimed. Books have been written about him in English and French and German. He even goes so far as to give us the author's and publishers' names – well-known live publishers who would surely never allow their names to be taken in vain. So it comes to this. If Strickland is a real man and this book a sort of guide to his works, it has its value; but if Mr Maugham is merely pulling our critical leg it will not do. Then, we are not told enough. We must be shown something of the workings of his mind; we must have some comment of his upon what he feels, fuller and more exhaustive than his perpetual: 'Go to hell.' It is simply essential that there should be some quality in him revealed to us that we may love, something that will stop us for ever from crying: 'If you have to be so odious before you can paint bananas – pray leave them unpainted.' . . .

This strange story is related by a friend of Mrs Strickland's, a young, rather priggish author, who is sent over to Paris after the first tragedy to discover with whom Strickland has eloped and whether he can be induced to return.

> 'You won't go back to your wife?' I said at last.
> 'Never.'
> ' ... She'll never make you a single reproach.'
> 'She can go to hell.'
> 'You don't care if people think you an utter blackguard? You don't care if she and her children have to beg their bread?'
> 'Not a damn.'

That is very typical of their conversations together. Indeed, the young man confesses that if Strickland is a great deal more articulate than that, he has put the words into his mouth – divined them from his gestures. 'From his own conversation I was able to glean nothing.' And 'his real life consisted of dreams and of tremendously hard work.' But where are the dreams? Strickland gives no hint of them; the young man makes no attempt to divine them. 'He asked nothing from his fellows except that they should leave him alone. He was single-hearted in his aim, and to pursue it he was willing to sacrifice not only himself – many can do that – but others ... ' But what does the sacrifice matter if you do not care a rap whether the creature on the altar is a little horned ram or your only beloved son?

The one outstanding quality in Strickland's nature seems to have been his contempt for life and the ways of life. But contempt for life is not to be confused with liberty, nor can the man whose weapon it is fight a tragic battle or die a tragic death. If to be a great artist were to push over everything that comes in one's way, topple over the table, lunge out right and left like a drunken man in a café and send the pots flying, then Strickland was a great artist. But great artists are not drunken men; they are men who are divinely sober. They know that the moon can never be bought for sixpence, and that liberty is only a profound realization of the greatness of the dangers in their midst.

> *Shows traces of hurry, and at the end,*
> *is pompous!*

Review of Kew Gardens[25] *by Virginia Woolf*
('A Short Story', 13 June 1919; in full)

If it were not a matter to sigh over, it would be almost amusing to remember how short a time has passed since Samuel Butler advised the budding author to keep a note-book. What would be the author's reply to such counsel nowadays but an amused smile: 'I keep nothing else!' True; but if we remember rightly, Samuel Butler goes a little further; he suggests that the note-book should be kept in the pocket, and that is what the budding author finds intolerably hard. Up till now he has been so busy growing and blowing that his masterpieces still are unwritten, but there are the public waiting, gaping. Hasn't he anything to offer before they wander elsewhere? Can't he startle their attention by sheer roughness and crudeness and general slapdashery? Out comes the note-book and the deed is done. And since they find its contents absolutely thrilling and satisfying, is it to be wondered at that the risk of producing anything bigger, more solid, and more positive – is not taken? The note-books of young writers are their laurels; they prefer to rest on them. It is here that one begins to sigh, for it is here that the young author begins to swell and to demand that, since he has chosen to make his note-books his All, they shall be regarded as of the first importance, read with a deadly seriousness and acclaimed as a kind of new Art – the art of not taking pains, of never wondering why it was one fell in love with this or that, but contenting oneself with the public's dreary interest in promiscuity.

Perhaps that is why one feels that Mrs Virginia Woolf's story belongs to another age. It is so far removed from the note-book literature of our day, so exquisite an example of love at second sight. She begins where the others leave off, entering Kew Gardens, as it were, alone and at her leisure when their little first screams of excitement have died away and they have rushed afield to some new brilliant joy. It is strange how conscious one is, from the first paragraph, of this sense of leisure: her story is bathed in it as if it were a light, still and lovely, heightening the importance of everything, and filling all that is within her vision with that vivid, disturbing beauty that haunts the air the last moment before sunset or the first moment after dawn. Poise – yes, poise. Anything may happen; her world is on tiptoe.

This is her theme. In Kew Gardens there was a flower-bed full of red and blue and yellow flowers. Through the hot July afternoon men and women 'straggled past the flower-bed with a curiously irregular movement not unlike that of the white and blue butterflies who crossed the turf in zig-zag flights from bed to bed', paused for a moment, were 'caught' in its dazzling net, and then moved on again and were lost. The mysterious intricate life of the flower-bed goes on untouched by these odd creatures. A little wind moves, stirring the petals so that their colours shake on to the brown earth, grey of a pebble, shell of a snail, a raindrop, a leaf, and for a moment the secret life is half-revealed; then a wind blows again, and the colours flash in the air and there are only leaves and flowers ...

It happens so often – or so seldom – in life, as we move among the trees, up and down the known and unknown paths, across the lawns and into the shade and out again, that something – for no reason that we can discover – gives us pause. Why is it that, thinking back upon that July afternoon, we see so distinctly that flower-bed? We must have passed myriads of flowers that day; why do these particular ones return? It is true, we stopped in front of them, and talked a little and then moved on. But, though we weren't conscious of it at the time, something was happening – something ...

But it would seem that the author, with her wise smile, is as indifferent as the flowers to these odd creatures and their ways. The tiny rich minute life of a snail – how she describes it! the angular high-stepping green insect – how passionate is her concern for him! Fascinated and credulous, we believe these things are all her concern until suddenly with a gesture she shows us the flower-bed, growing, expanding in the heat and light, filling a whole world.

Review of The Arrow of Gold *by Joseph Conrad*
(extracts from 'A Backward Glance', 8 August 1919)

As we read Mr Conrad's latest published book we find ourselves wishing once again that it were a common practice among authors to let us know the year in which a book is begun and ended. This, of course, applies only to writers whose work does show very marked signs of progression, development and expansion. The others, that large band who will guarantee to produce the same thrill with variations for you once, twice, or thrice yearly, do not count. For their great aim is never to show a sign of change – to make their next novel as good as their last, but no better – to take their readers for an excursion, as it were, but always to put up at the same hotel, where they know the waiters' faces, and the way to the bathroom, and the shape of the biscuits that accompany the cheese.

But perhaps your real writer would retort that this was precisely the business of the critic – to be able to see, at a glance almost, what place this or that novel filled in the growing chain. Our reply would be that the spirit of the age is against us; it is an uneasy, disintegrating, experimental spirit, and there are moments, as, for instance, the moment after reading the *Arrow of Gold*, when it shakes us into wishing that Mr Conrad had just added those four figures, thereby putting out once and for all that tiny flicker of dismay.

But – away with it! It is impossible not to believe that he has had this particular novel in the cellar for a considerable time – this sweet, sparkling, heady mixture in the strange-shaped bottle with the fantastic label.[26] How does it stand being held up to the light, tasted, sipped, and compared with those dark foreign beverages with which he has made us so familiar?

The tale is told by a young man who confesses to being, at the time, 'inconceivably young – still beautifully unthinking – infinitely receptive'. Lonely and sober, at Carnival time in Marseilles he chums up with two remarkable gentlemen; one Captain Blunt, 'eminently elegant', and the other a robust, fair little man in clothes too tight for him, a Mr Mills. They are both connected with the plot to put Don Carlos on the throne of Spain – Blunt as a soldier, and Mills as a gun-runner; and the talk between these three comparative strangers is of the ship loaded with contraband which Mills brought from the Clyde, how it was chased by a republican gunboat and stranded, and whether it would be possible to escape the vigilance of the French Customs authorities and salve the cargo for the cause. The French Customs cannot be bribed, but a mere hint from high quarters ... and here Captain Blunt 'let fall casually the words, "She will manage it for you quite easily." ' 'She' is the *femme fatale*, the woman of all times, the Old Enchantress, the idol before whom no man can do aught but worship, the Eternal Feminine, Donna Rita, woman. . . .

The plot moves on. Blunt flashes his teeth, Mills disappears, Donna Rita's inscrutable maid grows in inscrutability, a group of preposterous creatures move within its circle – they are there – they are gone – Monsieur George succeeds in adventure and almost succeeds in love – until there is a crisis so fantastical that we cannot but fancy Mr Conrad of to-day smiling at its stage horrors. Out of the murderous clutch of a little man who loved her in her wild childhood and has haunted her ever since, a little man with whiskers 'black and cut somewhat in the shape of a shark's fin, and so very fine that the least breath of air animated them into a sort of playful restlessness', Monsieur George bears her away to a villa 'embowered in roses', and to six months of happy love. But then

Monsieur George is called upon to fight a duel with Captain Blunt, and when he recovers of his wound it is to find that the *femme fatale*, simply because she is a *femme fatale*, has forsaken him, leaving behind her for remembrance the arrow of gold.

This example of Mr Conrad in search of himself, Mr Conrad, a pioneer, surveying the rich untravelled forest landscape of his mind, is extraordinarily revealing. When we think of his fine economy of expression, his spare use of gesture, his power of conveying the mystery of another's being, and contrast it with:

> She listened to me, unreadable, unmoved, narrowed eyes, closed lips, slightly flushed face, as if carved six thousand years ago in order to fix for ever that something secret and obscure which is in all women. Not the gross immobility of a sphinx proposing roadside riddles, but the finer immobility, almost sacred, of a fateful figure seated at the very source of the passions that have moved men from the dawn of ages ...

– we are amazed to think of the effort it has cost him to clear that wild luxurious country and to build thereupon his dignified stronghold.

Review of Night and Day *by Virginia Woolf*
('A Ship Comes into the Harbour', 21 November 1919; in full)

There is at the present day no form of writing which is more eagerly, more widely discussed than the novel. What is its fate to be? We are told on excellent authority that it is dying; and on equally good authority that only now it begins to live. Reviewers might almost be divided into two camps. Present each camp with the same book, and from one there comes a shout of praise, from the other a chorus of blame, each equally loud, determined and limited. One would imagine from a reading of the press notices that never in the history of the world was there such a generous distribution of the divine fire together with such an overwhelming display of ignorance, stupidity and dreariness. But in all this division and confusion it would seem that opinion is united in declaring this to be an age of experiment. If the novel dies it will be to give way to some new form of expression; if it lives it must accept the fact of a new world.

To us who love to linger down at the harbour, as it were, watching the new ships being builded, the old ones returning, and the many putting out to sea, comes the strange sight of *Night and Day* sailing into port serene and resolute on a deliberate wind. The strangeness lies in her aloofness, her air of quiet perfection, her lack of any sign that she has made a perilous voyage – the absence of any scars. There she lies among the strange shipping – a tribute to civilization for our admiration and wonder.

It is impossible to refrain from comparing 'Night and Day' with the novels of Miss Austen. There are moments, indeed, when one is almost tempted to cry it Miss Austen up-to-date. It is extremely cultivated, distinguished and brilliant, but above all – deliberate. There is not a chapter where one is unconscious of the writer, of her personality, her point of view, and her control of the situation. We feel that nothing has been imposed on her: she has chosen her world, selected her principal characters with the nicest care, and having traced a circle round them so that they exist and are free within its confines, she has proceeded, with rare appreciativeness, to register her observations. The result is a very long novel, but we do not see how it could be otherwise. This leisurely progression is essential to its manner, nor could the reader, even if he would, drink such wine at a gulp. As in the case of Miss Austen's novels we fall under a little spell; it is as though, realizing our safety, we surrender ourselves to the author, confident that whatever she has to show us, and however strange it may appear, we shall not be frightened or shocked. Her creatures are, one might say, privileged; we can rely upon her fine mind to deliver them from danger, to temper the blow (if a blow must fall), and to see their way clear for them at the very last. It is the measure of Mrs Woolf's power that her 'happy ending' could never be understood as a triumph of the heart over the mind. But whereas Miss Austen's spell is as strong upon us as ever when the novel is finished and laid by, Mrs Woolf's loses something of its potency. What is it that carries us away? With Miss Austen, it is her feeling for life, and then her feeling for writing; but with Mrs Woolf these feelings are continually giving way the one to the other, so that the urgency of either is impaired. While we read we scarcely are aware which is uppermost; it is only afterwards, and, specially when recalling the minor characters, that we begin to doubt. Sally Seal of the Suffrage Society, Mr Clacton with his French novel, old Joan in her shabby dress, Mrs Denham peering among the cups and saucers: it is true that these characters are not in any high degree important – but how much life have they? We have the queer sensation that once the author's pen is removed from them they have neither speech nor motion, and are not to be revived again until she adds another stroke or two or writes another sentence beneath. Were they shadowy or vague this would be less apparent, but they are held within the circle of steady light in which the author bathes her world, and in their case the light seems to shine at them, but not through them.

Night and Day tells of Katharine Hilbery's attempt to reconcile the world of reality with what, for want of a better name, we call the dream world. She belongs to one of the most distinguished families in England. Her mother's father was that 'fairest flower that any family can boast' – a great poet. Katharine's father is an eminent man of letters, and she herself as an only child 'had some superior rank among all the cousins and connections'. Grave, beautiful, with a reputation for being eminently practical and sensible beyond her years, she keeps house for her parents in Chelsea, but this activity does not exhaust Katharine. She has her lonely life remote from the drawing-room in Cheyne Walk, and it is divided between dreams 'such as the taming of wild ponies on the American prairies, or the conduct of a vast ship in a hurricane round a promontory of rock', and the study of mathematics. This last is her half-conscious but profound protest against the family tradition, against the making of phrases and (what Mrs Woolf rather curiously calls) 'the confusion, agitation and vagueness of the finest prose'.

But it is only after she has contracted an engagement which is in every way highly suitable with William Rodney, a scholar whose knowledge of Shakespeare, of Latin and Greek, is not to be disputed or denied, that she realizes in so doing she has in some mysterious way betrayed her dream world – the lover on the great horse riding by the seashore and the leaf-hung forests. Must life be for ever this lesser thing, this world as we know it, shapely, polished and secure? Katharine had no impulse to write poetry, yet it was the poet in her that made her see in Ralph Denham the man for whom she could feel that strange great passion which is like a fire lighting up the two worlds with the one exultant flame ...

It would be interesting to know how far Mrs Woolf has intended to keep this dream world of Katharine's and of Ralph's a deep secret from her readers. We are told that it is there, and we believe it; yet would not our knowledge of these two be wonderfully increased if there were something more than these suggestions that are like delicate veils hiding the truth? ...

As for the real world, the world of Mr and Mrs Hilbery, William Rodney, Cassandra Otway – there we appreciate to the full the author's exquisite generosity. It is so far away, so shut and sealed from us to-day. What could be more remote than the house at Cheyne Walk, standing up in the night, with its three long windows gilded with light, its drawn velvet curtains, and the knowledge that within a young creature is playing Mozart, Mrs Hilbery is wishing there were more young men like Hamlet, and Katharine and Rodney are faced by the incredible sight of Denham, outside in the dark, walking up and down ...

We had thought that this world was vanished for ever, that it was impossible to find on the great ocean of literature a ship that was unaware of what has been happening. Yet here is *Night and Day* fresh, new, and exquisite, a novel in the tradition of the English novel. In the midst of our admiration it makes us feel old and chill: we had never thought to look upon its like again!

See the following letters to J. M. Murry for evidence of KM's agitation over this review, and for her private opinions about the novel.

I am doing Virginia for this week's novel. I don't like it, Boge. My private opinion is that it is a lie in the soul. The war never has been: that is what its message is. I don't want (G. forbid!) mobilisation and the violation of Belgium, but the novel can't just leave the war out. There *must* have been a change of heart. It is really fearful to see the 'settling down' of human beings. I feel in the *profoundest* sense that nothing can ever be the same – that, as artists, we are traitors if we feel otherwise: we have to take it into account and find new expressions, new moulds for our new thoughts and feelings. Is this exaggeration? What *has* been stands, but Jane Austen could not write *Northanger Abbey* now – or if she did, I'd have none of her.

There is a trifling scene in Virginia's book where a charming young creature in a light fantastic attitude plays the flute: it positively frightens me – to realise this *utter coldness* and indifference. But I will be very careful and do my best to be dignified and sober. Inwardly I despise them all for a set of *cowards*. We have to face our war. They won't.   (10 November 1919)

But seriously, Bogey, the more I read the more I feel all these novels will not do. After them I'm a swollen sheep looking up who is not fed. And yet I feel one can lay down no rules. It's not in the least a question of material or style or plot. I can only think in terms like 'a change of heart'. I can't imagine how after the war these men can

pick up the old threads as though it had never been. Speaking to *you*
I'd say we have died and live again. How can that be the same life? It
doesn't mean that life is the less precious or that 'the common things
of light and day' are gone. They are not gone, they are intensified,
they are illumined. Now we know ourselves for what we are. In a
way it's a tragic knowledge: it's as though, even while we live again,
we face death. But *through Life*: that's the point. We see death in life
as we see death in a flower that is fresh unfolded. Our hymn is to the
flower's beauty: we would make that beauty immortal because we
know. Do you feel like this – or otherwise – or how?

But, of course, you don't imagine I mean by this knowledge
let-us-eat-and-drink-ism. No, I mean 'deserts of vast eternity'. But
the difference between you and me is (perhaps I'm wrong) I couldn't
tell anybody *bang out* about those deserts: they are my secret. I might
write about a boy eating strawberries or a woman combing her hair
on a windy morning, and that is the only way I can ever mention
them. But they *must* be there. Nothing less will do. They can
advance and retreat, curtsey, caper to the most delicate airs they
like, but I am bored to Hell by it all. Virginia, *par exemple.*

(16 November 1919)

See also this extract from a letter of J. M. Murry to KM, regarding her
review:

Your review of Virginia arrived this morning in time for the number.
I think it is (sans blague) one of the very finest reviews I have ever
read. The exquisite poise & beauty of the opening; the mastery with
which you give the whole quality & limitation of the book; the
sureness of your touch; and – above all & again – the beauty of the
writing, make it indisputably a masterpiece in the genre.

It was 6 lines [too] long. As you know the paper is all made up by
Wednesday morning, and it's impossible to allow more than a page.
I never had such anguish in trying to get 6 lines out of a piece of copy
before. I took them out of the description of Katharine's duties at
home. I felt that those could be spared best. They seemed to contain
less of what was specifically yours – the light which you cast on the
book, wh: was a real, suave, delicate, unfaltering light.

(19 November 1919)

See finally 'A Tragic Comedienne', an unsigned review of *Night and Day*
from the *Nation* (15 May 1920). Anthony Alpers suggests that this review too

is by KM, 'a second attempt by KM to review the book without constraint'.[27] Certainly the review is more direct, though not quite as impressive as the one published in the *Athenaeum*. It is printed here in full.

Imagine a comedy, witty in phrase, exquisitely 'mounted', stage-managed so that all its scenes move with a life-like ease – and wrongly cast, and you will have some idea of the faults and virtues of Mrs Woolf's novel. It used to be said of Mrs Siddons that she drank tea as if she were drinking poison. That did not mean that Mrs Siddons was not a wonderful person; it meant that a tea-party was not her proper environment. We find the same fault with Mrs Woolf's heroine, Katherine Hilberry [*sic*]. She is a Webster strayed among Sheridans, a Balzac among Jane Austens. She is too great for her company, altogether too beautiful and remarkable for them. She spoils the perfection of the whole. She is wasted. That is the queer thing about *Night and Day*, its chief fault is also its greatest ornament. Katherine Hilberry moves through the sheltered places of the book with an air of tragedy. Her stars, we feel, shine darkly over her. It is not towards the defection of a life-long admirer whom she does not love and a match with a young man of low origin that she is moving.

Mrs Woolf tells us that story as hers, but we do not believe it. We see her in Mrs Woolf's pages as we might see her in the street, and just as we should remember her and speculate about her there, so we do here. What Mrs Woolf tells us in her 500 pages does not satisfy us. About the rest of the cast we have not these doubts. Mrs Hilberry, that charming amateur of every pleasant thing, with her amiability, her ineffective brilliance, her sweetness of soul, thought and behaved exactly as Mrs Woolf says she did. Mr Hilberry, with his handsome profile, his beard and his punctiliousness, is as real as if we were sitting in the same drawing-room with him. But Katherine's cloak, her ruby ring, her beauty and softness as of 'a large snowy owl', her dislike of books (how keenly one sympathizes with that trait), her desire for such firmly ordered things as mathematics and astronomy, the wild, romantic country of sea and forest to which she hastened in her day dreams – these we maintain tended to other things than even the stormiest tea-cups. To say that character is destiny is usually to say that two interesting things have become one dull thing. In Katherine's case it would have been easy to make two interesting things into a third interesting thing. We do not believe that the happenings here were her destiny. We feel, in this book, that Mrs Woolf has deliberately restrained her own tragic powers. She has created a vessel for them in spite of herself as it were, and she has left it unfilled. In *The Voyage Out* she gave us a death that we remember as one of the few moving scenes in modern fiction, that we remember better than most of the moving scenes that have enveloped us in life. It appears in our memory as a woman standing by a table, picking up a letter and dropping it again. That woman and that attitude were significant. In *Night and Day* the woman and the attitude are there; but Mrs Woolf has refrained from making them significant. She has turned the panther of her natural gift into a plump, domestic pussy-cat. She could more fitly have called her book 'Nightlight and Day', for the intensity and the fears of night have been shut out.

Mrs Woolf has written a delightful comedy; but her leading lady's heels should have been a little lighter for her part. When Katherine is on the stage we look for something sadder and stranger that her promise yields. There is a scene, for instance, of an interfering aunt's coming in by the backstairs to warn Katherine that the man to whom she is engaged is paying attention to her friend Cassandra. The emotion that this news arouses must, in the circumstance of the novel, be quite trivial. Rodney, the fiancé, is a ridiculous person whose being fallen in love with by anyone seems to us highly improbable. Katherine has become accustomed to his devotion, but the prospect of marriage with him is so unattractive that she assists him in transferring his affections to her friend. For an aunt to interfere in anything is bound to be annoying; but Mrs Woolf banks the fires of feeling out of all proportion to the size of her emotional room. Katherine, arranging her flowers in the sunlight and hearing this disagreeable news, should, we feel, be a deceived wife, a superseded mistress, above all else, a creature wounded to the heart. As it is we have the sensation, as we read, of the people who found, instead of the Humbert millions, a button in the safe.

This defect keeps us from being absorbed and carried away by the story. We can put the book down at any moment without impatience. We take it up again, however, with unfailing pleasure and admiration. Its innumerable details reveal themselves to us with ever-increasing delight. Mrs Woolf writes of landscape as Dorothy Wordsworth wrote of it. She paints in words with the freshness and precision of a pre-Raphaelite. She has chosen beautiful scenes to describe and she describes them beautifully. Candle-lit interiors, Kew Gardens, the river, London at night, country fields – if it were for its landscape alone *Night and Day* would be a book to praise and treasure. Its beauties are never dragged in or irrelevant. They are part of the pattern. Her people are interwoven with the visual beauty of the world. Mrs Woolf sees what she describes with scientific exactness and poetic rapture. She sees with equal clearness the emotions and ideas that flit through the human soul. She contrives to give to each of her characters a private spiritual life as well as a public one. They speculate about themselves, about one another; they appear to us as they are in their own eyes and in other people's. Ralph Denham, with his love for Katherine, is perhaps the most alive person in the book. He has a real existence for us. He is not a type, and as an individual he is rare – we have known young men who kept accounts and young men who gave silver to beggars; and we have not commonly found these two excellences in one body – but he is convincing. The fact that he is kind to animals is no less a characteristic of his than the fact that he feels hostile and resentful among his social superiors, and that his consciousness of greater mental vigor makes him long to bully them.

Night and Day is, above all things, the expression of an original and powerful mind. We rejoice more in the accessibility of Mrs Woolf's mind than in her story. She has, we think, in writing pure comedy deliberately sacrificed part of her genius. She has entered into the artist's struggle with her material with one hand tied behind her. Luckily in writing this handicap matters less than in some other occupations. Mrs Woolf's talent is so splendid in its richness and fine in its quality that half of it will go as far as the talents of ten less gifted writers. There is one anachronism in *Night and Day* to point out however; is it possible to buy buns for the bears at the Zoo on Sunday?

Review of Interim[28] *by Dorothy Richardson*
(extracts from 'Dragonflies', 9 January 1920)

Who can tell, watching the dragonfly, at what point in its swift angular flight it will suddenly pause and hover, quivering over this or that? The strange little jerk – the quivering moment of suspension – we might almost fancy they were the signs of a minute inward shock of recognition felt by the dragonfly. 'There is something here; something here for me. What is it?' it seems to say. And then, at the same instant, it is gone. Away it darts, glancing over the deep pool until another floating flower or golden bud or tangle of shadowy weed attracts it, and again it is still, curious, hovering over ...

But this behaviour, enchanting though it may be in the dragonfly, is scarcely adequate when adopted by the writer of fiction. Nevertheless, there are certain modern authors who do not appear to recognize its limitations. For them the whole art of writing consists in the power with which they are able to register that faint inward shock of recognition. Glancing through life they make the discovery that there are certain experiences which are, as it were, peculiarly theirs. There is a quality in the familiarity of these experiences or in their strangeness which evokes an immediate mysterious response – a desire for expression. But now, instead of going any further, instead of attempting to relate their 'experiences' to life or to see them against any kind of background, these writers are, as we see them, content to remain in the air, hovering over, as if the thrilling moment were enough and more than enough. Indeed, far from desiring to explore it, it is as though they would guard the secret for themselves as well as for us, so that when they do dart away all is as untouched, as unbroken as before.

But what is the effect of this kind of writing upon the reader? How is he to judge the importance of one thing rather than another if each is to be seen in isolation? And is it not rather cold comfort to be offered a share in a secret on the express understanding that you do not ask what the secret is – more especially if you cherish the uncomfortable suspicion that the author is no wiser than you, that the author is in love with the secret and would not discover it if he could? . . .

Interim, which is the latest slice from the life of Miriam Henderson, might almost be described as a nest of short stories. There is Miriam Henderson, the box which holds them all, and really it seems there is no end to the number of smaller boxes that Miss Richardson can make her contain. But *Interim* is a very little one indeed. In it Miriam is enclosed in a Bloomsbury boarding-house, and though she receives, as usual, shock after shock of inward recognition, they are produced by such things as well-browned mutton, gas jets, varnished wallpapers. Darting through life, quivering, hovering, exulting in the familiarity and the strangeness of all that comes within her tiny circle, she leaves us feeling, as before, that everything being of equal importance to her, it is impossible that everything should not be of equal unimportance.

Review of The Rescue[29] *by Joseph Conrad*
(extract from 'Mr Conrad's New Novel', 2 July 1920)

The writer who has achieved more than a common popularity, who has been recognized as one of the very few whose place is not in the crowded and jostled front rank but a delightful airy perch among the mountains, is to be envied – and not to be envied. The distinguished position has its special drawbacks. Whether it is the effect upon him of the rarefied air, or of the dignified solitude, or of the cloud interposing and obscuring the smaller eminences, the valleys and the plains from his, at one time, eager gaze, we do not know, but the books which come down to us from the mountains are no longer the books they were. They are variations upon the themes that made him famous; they are 'safe' books, guaranteed to leave unchallenged the masterpiece that put him there. Who would tempt Providence twice? And so from timidity or pride, from poverty of imagination, or a high sense of his 'unique' duty, he continues to repeat himself, and it is only his memory which is in our flowing cups richly remembered.

Mr Joseph Conrad is a remarkable exception to this lamentable case. Although he has long been recognized as one of our first writers to-day, he has never yet succeeded in satisfying our curiosity. We are always waiting for the next book, always imagining that in the new book he will reveal himself fully: there will come floating in, on a full tide, his passion for the sea, his sense of style, his spectacular view of the universe, his romantic vision of the hearts of men, and we shall have the whole of Conrad – his measure – the bounds of his experience. These are large demands, but we do not think there is any doubt that they are more than satisfied by the appearance of *The Rescue*. This fascinating book revives in us the youthful feeling that we are not so much reading a story of adventure as living in and through it, absorbing it, making it our own. This feeling is not wholly the result of the method, the style which the author has chosen; it arises more truly from the quality of the emotion in which the book is steeped. What that emotion is it were hard to define; it is, perhaps, a peculiar responsive sensitiveness to the significance of everything, down to the slightest detail that has a place in his vision. Even in the sober low-toned beginning the author succeeds in conveying a warning as of an approaching storm; it is as though the silence was made to bear a mysterious implication. And in this heightened, quickened state of awareness we are made conscious of his passionate insistence upon the importance of extracting from the moment every drop of life that it contains, wherewith to nourish his adventure.

Review of a reissue of Esther Waters *by George Moore* (*'Esther Waters Revisited'*, *6 August 1920; in full*)

Although conversation of the kind is seldom very fruitful, while young writers gather together it would be hard to find a topic more suited to their enthusiasm than 'Who are, when all is said and done, our best writers to-day, and why do we think so?' Present-day literature consists almost entirely of poetry and the novel, and when it is the latter which has been under discussion; when there has been a furious rage of condemning, admiring, prophesying, upholding; when all is over and the participants have distributed to their satisfaction the laurel and the bay, it is not uncommon to hear, from a corner, an American or a French voice upraised: 'But what about Mr George Moore?' Of course; how strange! How difficult it is to explain how so distinguished a figure in modern letters comes to be forgotten! And even when we recall him to memory do we not see him dim, pale, shadowy, vanishing round this corner, disappearing behind that door, almost in the rôle of expert private detective to his novels rather than author, ... This, too, in spite of his detachment and candour, taking into account the delighted retracing, retracking himself down, so to say, for which he is famous. We have no other writer who is so fond of talking of his art. So endless is his patience, so sustained his enthusiasm, we have the feeling that he cannot refrain from confiding in the stupid public, simply because he cannot keep silent. And yet – there is the strange fact. While we are engaged in reading Mr George Moore's novels he is 'there,' but once they are put back on the shelves he has softly and silently vanished away until he is heard of again.

The publication of a new edition of *Esther Waters* provides an opportunity for seeking to understand this curious small problem. It is generally agreed that this novel is the best he has written, and the author himself has expressed his delight in it – 'the book that among all other books I should have cared most to write, and to have written it so much better than I ever dreamed it could be written'. *Esther Waters* is, on the face of it, a model novel. Having read it carefully and slowly – we defy anyone to race along or skip – from cover to cover, we are left feeling that there is not a page, paragraph, sentence, word, that is not the right, the only possible page, paragraph, sentence, word. The more we look into it, the more minute our examination, the deeper grows our amazement at the amount of sheer labour that has gone to its execution. Nothing from: 'She stood on the platform watching the receding train', until the last pale sentence, the last quiet closing chord is taken for granted. How is it possible for Mr George Moore to have gained such precise knowledge of the servants' life in Esther's first place unless he disguised himself as a kitchen-maid and plunged his hands into the cauliflower water? There is not a detail of the kitchen and pantry life at Woodview that escapes his observation; the description of the bedroom shared by Esther and the housemaid Margaret is as complete as though the author were preparing us for some sordid crime to be committed there. And this intensely scrupulous method, this dispassionate examination is continued without a break in the even flow of the narrative. Turn to the page of the heroine's seduction:

The wheat stacks were thatching, and in the rickyard, in the carpenter's shop, and in the warm valleys, listening to the sheep-bells tinkling, they often lay together talking of love and marriage till one evening, putting his pipe aside, William threw his arm round her, whispering she was his wife.

'Putting his pipe aside!' Could anything express a nicer control, a cooler view of the emotional situation? It is only equalled by: 'Soon after thoughts betook themselves on their painful way, and the stars were shining when he followed her across the down, beseeching her to listen.' It comes to this. There is not, in retrospect, one single page which is not packed as tightly as it can hold with whatever can be recorded. When we follow Esther to London here is the crown of the book. It is the London of that particular time preserved whole, a true 'London of the water's edge' – a London of theatres, music-halls, wine-shops, public-houses. And it is the scene of the struggle of Esther Waters to be a good woman and to bring up her child against fearful odds. The life of a general servant – how sordid, how vulgar, how ignoble! What a trapesing up and down stairs and a turning-out of ugly rooms! Mr Moore spares us none of it, and when her 'luck changes', and, married to the man who seduced her, Esther has a home of her own, it is the centre of a low-class gambling lot. Could all this be more faithfully described than the author has described it?

Could it possibly be more complete, more probable? The technique is so even, it is as though a violinist were to play the whole concerto in one stroke of the bow.

And yet we would say without hesitation that *Esther Waters* is not a great novel, and never could be a great novel, because it has not, from first to last, the faintest stirring of the breath of life. It is as dry as the remainder biscuit after a voyage. In a word it has no emotion. Here is a world of objects accurately recorded, here are states of mind set down, and here, above all, is that good Esther whose faith in her Lord is never shaken, whose love for her child is never overpowered – and who cares?

> In the last year Jackie had taken much and given nothing. But when she opened Mrs Lewis's door he came running to her, calling her Mummie; and the immediate preference he showed for her, climbing on her knees instead of Mrs Lewis's, was a fresh sowing of love in the mother's heart.

Do we not feel that to be the detective rather than the author writing? It is an arid, sterile statement. Or this:

> But when they came to the smooth wide … roads … she put him down, and he would run along ahead, crying, 'Tum for a walk, Mummie, tum along', and his little feet went so quickly beneath his frock that it seemed as if he were on wheels. She followed, often forced to break into a run, tremulous lest he should fall …

The image of the little feet on wheels is impossibly flat and cold, and 'tremulous' is never the word for Esther – 'trembling' or 'all of a tremble' – the other word reveals nothing. What it comes to is that we believe that emotion is essential to a work of art; it is that which makes a work of art a unity. Without emotion writing is dead; it becomes a record instead of a revelation, for the sense of revelation comes from that emotional reaction which the artist felt and was impelled to communicate. To contemplate the object, to let it make its own impression – which is Mr Moore's way in *Esther Waters* – is not enough. There must be an initial emotion felt by the writer, and all that he sees is saturated in that emotional quality. It alone can give incidence and sequence, character and background, a close and intimate unity. Let the reader turn to the scene where Sarah gets drunk because her horse has lost. It is a fearful scene, and so closely described that we might be at her elbow. But now Sarah speaks, now Esther, now William, and all is as cold and toneless as if it were being read out of that detective's notebook again. It is supremely good evidence; nothing is added, nothing is taken away, but we forget it as soon as it is read for we have been given nothing to remember. Fact succeeds fact, and with the reflection that Esther and her husband 'fell asleep, happy in each other's love, seeming to find new bonds of union in pity for their friend's misfortune', the scene closes. Is that all? No wonder we forget Mr George Moore. To praise such work as highly as he does is to insult his readers' intelligence.

Review of The Story of the Siren *by E. M. Forster*
('Throw them Overboard', 13 August 1920; in full)[30]

The delightful event of a new story by Mr E. M. Forster sets us wishing that it had not been so long to wait between his last novel and his new book. He is one of the very few younger English writers whose gifts are of a kind to compel our curiosity as well as our admiration. There is in all his novels a very delicate sense of the value of atmosphere, a fine precision of expression, and his appreciation of the uniqueness of the characters he portrays awakens in him a kind of special humour, half whimsical, half sympathetic. It is in his best-known novel, *Howard's End*, that he is most successful in conveying to the reader the effect of an assurance that he possesses a vision which reigns within; but in *Howard's End*, though less than elsewhere, we are teased by the feeling, difficult to define, that he has by no means exerted the whole of his imaginative power to create that world for his readers. This, indeed, it is which engages our curiosity. How is it that the writer is content to do less than explore his own delectable country?

There is a certain leisureliness which is of the very essence of Mr Forster's style – a constant and fastidious choosing of what the unity shall be composed – but while admitting the necessity for this and the charm of it, we cannot deny the danger to the writer of drifting, of finding himself beset with fascinating preoccupations which tempt him to put off or even to turn aside from the difficulties which are outside his easy reach. In the case of Mr Forster the danger is peculiarly urgent because of his extreme reluctance to – shall we say? – commit himself wholly. By letting himself be borne along, by welcoming any number of diversions, he can still appear to be a stranger, a wanderer, within the boundaries of his own country, and so escape from any declaration of allegiance. To sum this up as a cynical attitude on the part of the author would be, we are convinced, to do him a profound wrong. Might it not be that this conscience is over-developed, that he is himself his severest critic, his own reader full of eyes? So aware is he of his sensitiveness, his sense of humour, that they are become two spectators who follow him wherever he goes, and are for ever on the look-out for a display of feeling ...

It was the presence of 'my aunt and the chaplain' on the first page of *The Story of the Siren* which suggested the tentative explanation above. The teller of the story is in a boat outside a little grotto on a great sunlit rock in the Mediterranean. His notebook has dropped over the side.

> 'It is such a pity', said my aunt, 'that you will not finish your work at the hotel. Then you would have been free to enjoy yourself and this would never have happened.'
> 'Nothing of it but will change into something rich and strange', warbled the chaplain . . . .

It would be extremely unfair to suggest that Mr Forster's novels are alive with aunts and black with chaplains, and yet these two figures are so extraordinarily familiar, that we caught ourselves unjustifiably wondering why there must always be, on every adventure, an aunt and a warbling chaplain. Why must they always be there in the boat, bright, merciless, clad from head to foot in the armour of efficiency?

It is true that in this particular story the hero escapes from them almost immediately. He and Giuseppe are left on a rock outside the cave, so that the boatman may dive and recover his notebook. But the mischief is done. All through the enchanting story told by Giuseppe after the book is rescued, we seem to hear a ghostly accompaniment. They 'had been left together in a magic world, apart from all the commonplaces that are called reality, a world of blue whose floor was the sea and whose walls and roof of rock trembled with the sea's reflections'; but something has happened there which should not have happened there – so that the radiance is faintly dimmed, and that beautiful trembling blue is somehow just blurred, and the voice of Giuseppe has an edge on it which makes it his voice for the foreigner: the aunt and the chaplain, in fine, are never to be wholly got rid of. By this we do not wish to suggest for one moment that the key of the story should be changed, should be pitched any lower. It is exquisitely right. But we do wish Mr Forster would believe that his music is too good to need any bush.

Review of Three Lives[31] *by Gertrude Stein*
(extracts from 'Some New Thing', 15 October 1920)

Miss Gertrude Stein has discovered a new way of writing stories. It is just to keep right on writing them. Don't mind how often you go back to the beginning, don't hesitate to say the same thing over and over again – people are always repeating themselves – don't be put off if the words sound funny at times: just keep right on, and by the time you've done writing you'll have produced your effect. Take, for instance, the first story of the good Anna who managed the whole little house for Miss Matilda and the three dogs and the underservant as well. For five years Anna managed the little house for Miss Matilda. In those five years there were four underservants. 'The one that came first … ' She was succeeded by Molly; and when Molly left, old Katy came in every day to help Anna with her work. When Miss Matilda went away this summer 'old Katy was so sorry, and on the day that Miss Matilda went, old Katy cried hard for many hours … When Miss Matilda early in the fall came to her house again old Katy was not there.' At last Anna heard of Sally. . . .

Now that simple German way of telling about those simple German women may be very soothing – very pleasant – but let the reader go warily, warily with Melanctha. We confess we read a good page or two before we realized what was happening. Then the dreadful fact dawned. We discovered ourselves reading *in syncopated time*. Gradually we heard in the distance, and then coming uncomfortably near, the sound of banjos, drums, bones, cymbals and voices. The page began to rock. To our horror we found ourselves silently singing:

> Was it true what Melanctha had said that night to him? Was it true he was the one had made all this trouble for them? Was it true he was the only one who always had had wrong ways in him? Waking or sleeping, Jeff now always had this torment …

Those who have heard the Southern Orchestra sing 'It's me – it's me – it's me' or 'I got a robe' will understand what we mean.

'Melanctha' is negro music with all its maddening monotony done into prose; it is writing in real rag-time. Heaven forbid Miss Stein should become a fashion!

Reviews of In Chancery *by John Galsworthy and* The Age of Innocence
by Edith Wharton
(extracts from 'Family Portraits', 10 December 1920)

In his latest novel, which is a continuation of the Forsyte Saga, Mr John Galsworthy gives the impression of being in his real right element. There is a peculiar note, a mixture of confidence and hospitality, struck in the first chapter, which seems to come from the happy author warming himself at a familiar hearth. Here, in the very bosom of the Forsyte family, if any man is at home, he is that man. Its ramifications have no terrors for him; on the contrary, the quick, searching, backward glance he takes before setting out upon this book is yet long enough to be a kind of basking which extends to the cousin furthest removed.

A swollen flood of novels has flowed under the bridge since the days of our enthusiasm for *The Man of Property* – that large family piece, admirably composed, closely packed, and firmly related to a background which was never decoration only. *In Chancery* is less solid as a whole – the shell-pink azaleas escape the control of Soames' conservatory and flower a trifle too freely, as they are also a trifle too shell-pink; the tone is softer. It is not because the author is regarding his subject from another angle, but because all that remains from the deep vein of irony in *The Man of Property* is a faint ironic tinge. In *The Man of Property* what the author made us feel the Forsyte family lacked was imagination; in this new novel we feel it still, but we are not at all certain the author intends us to. He has, as it were, exchanged one prize for another – in gaining the walls he has lost his vision of the fortress. It is a very great gift for an author to be able to project himself into the hearts and minds of his characters – but more is needed to make a great creative artist; he must be able, with equal power, to withdraw, to survey what is happening – and from an eminence. But Mr Galsworthy is so deeply engaged, immersed and engrossed in the Forsyte family that he loses his freedom. He can see Soames and James and the two Bayswater Road ancients with intense vividness; he can tell us all about them – but not all there is to know. Why is this? Is it not because, *au fond*, he distrusts his creative energy? There is no question of a real combat between it and his mind; his mind is master. Hence we have a brilliant display of analysis and dissection, but without any 'mystery', any unplumbed depth to feed our imagination upon. The Forsyte men are so completely life-size, so bound within the crowns of their hats and the soles of their shoes, that they are almost something less than men. We do not doubt for a moment that it has been the aim of the author to appeal to the imagination; but so strong is the imposition of his mind that the appeal stops short at the senses. Take, for example, the character of old James Forsyte. Is it not amazing how he comes before us so that we see him, hear him, smell him, know his ways, his tricks, his habits as if he were our grandfather? Yet when we think of him – is it as standing at the window of his house watching the funeral of the old Queen, watching his own funeral and the funeral of his time – or as having his few last hairs stroked by Emily with a pair of silver brushes? These events should be of equal importance, at least; but they are not; the hair-brushing is easily first; and the author dwells on it with loving persistence until he almost succeeds in turning James into a lean, nervous, old, old, dog. Or take the occasion when young Val Dartie came face to face with his father, drunk, in the promenade of a music-hall. Before going out that evening he had asked his mother if he might have two plover's eggs when he came in. And when he does return, shocked, wretched, disenchanted with life, we find our concern for him overshadowed by those two plover's eggs laid out so temptingly with the cut bread and butter and 'just enough whisky in the decanter', and left to languish on the dining-room table. But perhaps these instances are too simple to illustrate our meaning. Let us examine for a moment the figure of Soames Forsyte, who is the hero of *In Chancery*. His desire to have a son makes him decide to divorce the faithless Irene and thus free himself to marry a healthy young Frenchwoman, the daughter of a restaurant keeper. Now Soames, the passionate, suppressed human animal desiring Irene still because she is unattainable, but satisfying himself with the French girl at the last, is as solid, as substantial as a mind could make him, but he is never real. He is flesh and blood with a strong dash of clay – long before he is a tormented man; and flesh and blood and clay he remains after the torment is on him. But there never comes that moment when the character is more than himself, so that we feel at the end that what should have happened to him never has happened. He is an appearance only – a lifelike image. . . .

In *The Age of Innocence*, a novel about the early seventies in New York, we receive the same impression that here is the element in which the author delights to breathe. The time and the scene together suit Mrs Wharton's talent to a nicety. To evoke the seventies is to evoke irony and romance at once, and to keep these two balanced by all manner of delicate adjustments is so much a matter for her skilful hand that it seems more like play than work. Like Mr Galsworthy's novel it is a family piece, but in *The Age of Innocence* the family comprises the whole of New York society. This remote, exclusive small world in itself is disturbed one day by the return of one of its prodigal daughters who begs to be taken back as though nothing had happened. What has happened is never quite clear, but it includes a fabulously rich villain of a Polish Count who is her husband and his secretary, who, rumour whispers, was all too ready to aid her escape. But the real problem which the family has to face is that Ellen Olenska has become that most mysterious creature – a European. She is dangerous, fascinating, foreign; Europe clings to her like a troubling perfume; her very fan beats 'Venice! Venice!' every diamond is a drop of Paris. Dare they accept her? The question is answered by a dignified compromise, and Ellen's farewell dinner-party before she leaves for Paris is as distinguished as she or the family could wish. These are what one might call the outer leaves of the story. Part them, and there is within another flower, warmer, deeper, and more delicate. It is the love-story of Newland Archer, a young man who belongs deeply to the family tradition, and yet at the same time finds himself wishing to rebel. The charm of Ellen is his temptation, and hard indeed he finds it not to yield. But that very quality in her which so allures him – what one might call her highly civilized appreciation of the exquisite difficulty of their position – saves them from themselves. Not a feather of dignity is ruffled; their parting is positively stately.

But what about us? What about her readers? Does Mrs Wharton expect us to grow warm in a gallery where the temperature is so sparklingly cool? We are looking at portraits – are we not? These are human beings, arranged for exhibition purposes, framed, glazed, and hung in the perfect light. They pale, they grow paler, they flush, they raise their 'clearest eyes,' they hold out their arms to each other 'extended, but not rigid,' and the voice is the voice of the portrait:

'What's the use – when will you go back?' he broke out, a great hopeless *How on earth can I keep you?* crying out to her beneath his words.

Is it – in this world – vulgar to ask for more? To ask that the feeling shall be greater than the cause that excites it, to beg to be allowed to share the moment of exposition (is not that the very moment that all our writing leads to?), to entreat a little wildness, a dark place or two in the soul?

We appreciate fully Mrs Wharton's skill and delicate workmanship; she has the situation in hand from the first page to the last; we realize how savage must sound our cry of protest, and yet we cannot help but make it; that after all we are not above suspicion – even the 'finest' of us!

KM's note on Aaron's Rod *(1920), appended by J. M. Murry to* Novels and Novelists[32]

There are certain things in this book I do not like. But they are not important, or really part of it. They are trivial, encrusted, they cling to it as snails to the underside of a leaf – no more, – and perhaps they leave a little silvery trail, a smear, that one shrinks from as from a kind of silliness. But apart from these things is the leaf, is the tree, firmly planted, deep thrusting, outspread, growing grandly, alive in every twig. All the time I read this book I felt it was feeding me.

Murry added this note in 1930, to 'give some record at least of [KM's] admiration for the work of D. H. Lawrence'. It should be recognised, however, that Murry was by this time engaged in writing his hagiography of D. H. Lawrence, *Son of Woman* (1931). To 'leave all fair', some of KM's criticism of Lawrence's work should also be included – for example, the following notes on *The Lost Girl*, and an extract from a 1921 letter to Sydney and Violet Schiff (extract not published by Murry).

I made these notes. Read them, will you?

'THE LOST GIRL'

It's important. It ought not to be allowed to pass.

The Times gave no inkling of what it was – never even hinted at its dark secret.

Lawrence denies his humanity. He denies the powers of the Imagination. He denies Life – I mean *human* life. His hero and heroine are non-human. They are animals on the prowl. They do not feel: they scarcely speak. There is not one memorable *word*. They submit to the physical response and for the rest go veiled – blind – *faceless – mindless*. This is the doctrine of mindlessness.

He says his heroine is extraordinary, and rails against the ordinary. Isn't that significant? But look at her. Take her youth – her thriving on the horse-play with the doctors. They might be beasts butting each other – no more. Take the scene where the hero throws her in the kitchen, possesses her, and she returns singing to the washing-up. It's a *disgrace*. Take the rotten rubbishy scene of the woman in labour asking the Italian into her bedroom. All false. All a pack of lies!

Take the nature-study at the end. It's no more than the grazing-place for Alvina and her sire. What was the 'green hellebore' to her? Of course, there is a great deal of racy, bright, competent writing in the early part – the 'shop' part. But it doesn't take a writer to tell all that.

The whole is false – *ashes*. The preposterous Indian troupe of four young men is – a fake. But how on earth he can keep it up is the problem. No, it's not. He has 'given way'. Why stop then? Oh, don't forget where Alvina feels '*a trill in her bowels*' and discovers herself with child. A TRILL – what does that mean? And why is it so peculiarly offensive from a man? Because it is *not on this plane* that the emotions of others are conveyed to our imagination. It's a kind of sinning against art.

Earth closets, too. Do they exist *quâ* earth closets? No. I might describe the queer noises coming from one when old Grandpa X was there – very strange cries and moans – and how the women who were washing stopped and shook their heads and pitied him and even the children didn't laugh. Yes, I can imagine that. But that's not the same as to build an earth-closet because the former one was so exposed. NO.

Am I prejudiced? Be careful. I feel privately as though Lawrence had possessed an animal and fallen under a curse. But I can't say that. All I know is, this is bad and ought not be allowed. I feel a horror of it – a shrinking. But that's not criticism. But here is life where one has blasphemed against the spirit of reverence.

(To J. M. Murry, December 1920)

What did you think of Lawrence in the *Dial*?[33] This last month isn't anything like so good; in fact when he gets on to the subject of *maleness* I lose all patience. What nonsense it all is – and he must know it is. His style changes; he can no longer write. *He begs the question.* I can't forgive him for that – its a sin.

(To Sydney and Violet Schiff, 3 December 1921)[34]

EUROPEAN NOVELISTS

Review of An Honest Thief: and Other Stories *by Fyodor Dostoevsky*
('Some Aspects of Dostoevsky', 28 November 1919; in full)

If we view it from a certain angle, it is not at all impossible to see in Dostoevsky's influence upon the English intellectuals of to-day the bones of a marvellously typical Dostoevsky novel. Supposing we select London for his small provincial town and his arrival for the agitating occurrence – could he himself exaggerate the discussions he has provoked, the expenditure of enthusiasm and vituperation, the mental running to and fro, the parties that have been given in his honour, the added confusion of several young gentlemen-writers declaring (in strict confidence) that they were the real Dostoevsky, the fascinating arguments as to whether or no he is greater than Jane Austen (what would Jane Austen have said to the bugs and the onions and the living in corners!), the sight of our young egoists puffing up like undismayed frogs, and of our superior inner circle who are not unwilling to admit that he has a considerable amount of crude strength before returning to their eighteenth-century muttons?

> Ohé Dostoevsky! Où est Dostoevsky?
> As-tu vu Dostoevsky?

Few indeed have so much as caught a glimpse of him. What would be the end of such a novel? His disappearance without doubt, leaving no trace but a feeling of, on the whole, very lively relief. For if we do not take him superficially, there is nothing for us to do but to take him terribly seriously, but to consider whether it is possible for us to go on writing our novels as if he never had been. This is not only a bitterly uncomfortable prospect; it is positively dangerous; it might very well end in the majority of our young writers finding themselves naked and shivering, without a book to clothe themselves in.

However, the danger is not a real one. There are signs that the fashion for him is on the wane. How otherwise can we interpret the avidity with which opinion seizes upon the less important, extravagant side of Dostoevsky, making much of it, making much of that and ignoring all else, than that it has had its fright, as it were, but now has been assured that the monster at the fair will not remain? But a remarkable feature of this parade of intellectual snobbishness, this laughing at the Russian giant, is that the writers appear to imagine that they laugh alone – that Dostoevsky had no idea of the exquisite humour of such a character as Stepan Trofimovitch, with his summer sickness, his breaking into French and his flight from civilization in a pair of top-boots, or that he regarded the super-absurdities of Prince K as other than quite normal characteristics. It is true that especially in some of the short stories we may find his sense of humour terribly jars on us, but that is when the humour is 'false'; it is exasperation disguised, an overwhelming nostalgia and bitterness disguised or an attempt at a sense of fun, in which never was man more wanting. Then, again, to laugh with Dostoevsky is not always a comfortable exercise for one's pride. For he has the – surely unpardonable – habit of describing at length, minutely, the infinitely preposterous state of mind of some poor wretch, not as though he were 'showing us a star', but with many a familiar nod and look in our direction, as much as to say: 'But you know yourself from your own experience what it is to feel *like this.*'

There is a story, 'An Unpleasant Predicament', in this collection which is a terrible example of this. It relates how a young general, exasperated by an evening with two elder colleagues whom he suspects of treating him like a schoolboy and laughing at him because of his belief in the new ideas, in humanity and sympathy with the working classes, yields to the temptation on the way home of putting himself to the test, of proving to his Amour Propre that he really is the fine fellow she thinks him to be. Why should he do anything so dangerous? He knows in his heart that he does not believe in any of these things, and yet isn't it possible for him to impose this idea of himself on anybody he chooses? And why should he not slay reality as an offering to his goddess? The revenge that reality takes upon Ivan Ilyitch Pralinsky is wild and violent and remote enough from our experience, and yet who can read it and not be overcome by the feeling that he understands only too well …

Perhaps Dostoevsky more than any other writer sets up this mysterious relationship with the reader, this sense of *sharing*. We are never conscious that he is writing at us or for us. While we read, we are like children to whom one tells a tale; we seem in some strange way to half-know what is coming and yet we do not know; to have heard it all before, and yet our amazement is none the less, and when it is over, it has become ours. This is especially true of the Dostoevsky who passes so unremarked – the childlike, candid, simple Dostoevsky who wrote 'An Honest Thief' and 'The Peasant Marly' and 'The Dream of a Queer Fellow'. These three wonderful stories have all the same quality, a stillness, a quiet that takes the breath. What have they to do with our time? They are full of the tragic candour of love. There is only one other man who could have written the death of Emelyanouska, as described by the poor little tailor:

> I saw Emelyanouska wanted to tell me something: he was trying to sit up, trying to speak, and mumbling something. He flushed red all over suddenly, looked at me ... then I saw him turn white again, whiter and whiter, and he seemed to sink away all in a minute. His head fell back, he drew one breath and gave up his soul to God.

Review of Old People and the Things that Pass *by Louis Couperus*[35]
(*extracts from 'A Foreign Novel', 12 December 1919*)

To those who have read *Small Souls* it will not come as a surprise that *Old People* is a study of a family. For one could not but feel after reading the former novel that the chief gift of the author must lie in his power of presenting a group of individuals each of whom, when seen apart, has a separate, different life, but all of whom when viewed together are found to be but the parts that go to make up one mysterious creature – the family. He proved indeed that small souls are not really capable of a separate existence; they may rebel against the family, defy it, laugh at it, but they are bound to recognize at the last that they cannot run away without longing to run back and that any step taken without its knowledge and approval is a step in the air.

There is passion in *Small Souls*, but the note is not deep or greatly troubled. It is full of gentle satire. Perhaps its quality is best expressed in the chapter where the little girl sits practising her scales, up and down, up and down the piano, always so carefully sounding the wrong note, on a windy morning. Her back is turned to the window. But outside everything is fresh and flying. Outside, in the sun and wind, life is on the wing, and inside there is the sound of doors shutting, the tinkle of the bell and the grown-up people walking up and down the stairs, talking as they go – and always very carefully sounding the wrong note ...

In *Old People* we have again a family, clinging to its houses, visiting, immensely absorbed in its family affairs, a whole little world of its own – but there the resemblance ends. The family in *Old People* is not united by small scandals, little jealousies, wars and spites; through it there flows, like a dark underground river, the memory of a crime ... . . .

These are the three ancient criminals, whom life will not let go. And while they wait and suffer there is a kind of terrible race going on between the desire of the children who know and who long for the old people to die before the secret is discovered, and the curiosity of those who do not know and who burn for the secret to be revealed before the old people die. Never once does the dark river burst above ground, but as the year deepens to winter it seems to grow loud and swollen and dreadful. Then quite suddenly, before the year is out, Mr Takma dies, and the old doctor, and last of all the old woman – and the river subsides.

Old People is one of those rare novels which, we feel, enlarge our experience of life. We are richer not only for having studied the marvellously drawn portraits of the three aged beings, but because we have marked their behaviour as they played their parts against this great half-hoop of darkening sky. But it is only when we think over the various members of that strange family that we realise how great is our gain. New people have appeared in that other world of ours, which sometimes seems so much more real and satisfying than this one; new characters to watch and ponder over and discover. That they have a life and being of their own we do not question; even that they 'go on' long after the book is finished – this we can believe. What is it then that differentiates these living characters from the book-bound creatures of even our brilliant modern English writers? Is it not that the former are seen ever and always in relation to life – not to a part of life, not to a set of society, but to the bounding horizon, life, and the latter are seen in relation to an intellectual idea of life? In this second case life is made to fit them; something is abstracted – something quite unessential – that they wouldn't in the least know what to do with ... and they are set in motion. But life cannot be made to 'fit' anybody, and the novelist who makes the attempt will find himself cutting something that gets smaller and smaller, finer and finer, until he must begin cutting his characters next to fit the thing he has made.

It is only by accepting life as M Couperus accepts it that the novelist is free – through his characters – to question it profoundly.

Review of The Garnet Bracelet *by Alexander Kuprin*
('Alexander Kuprin', 26 December 1919; in full)

In his introduction to this volume of short stories Mr Lyon Phelps, Professor of English Literature at Yale University, has seized the opportunity to inform, caution, and put 'right' American opinion upon the whole subject of Russian Literature. His manner in so doing is unfamiliar to English readers. It makes us feel that while we read we are, like Alice, dwindling away in height; by the end of the first page we are much too young even to attend a University; by the end of the second, and especially when that tiny little joke is popped into our baby mouths, we are of a size to spell out maxims at a learned knee:

A novel is not great simply because it is written in the Russian language, nor because its author has a name difficult to pronounce.

Or:

A slavish – no pun intended – adoration of Russian novels is not itself an indication of critical intelligence.

Or:

A pessimist is not necessarily a profound thinker, nor is uncleanness in itself a sign of virility.

But surely Mr Phelps exaggerates the extreme innocence of American literary opinion; he must surely be mistaken in not realizing that it has long cut down these modest flowers of thought with its little hatchet. Nevertheless even Kuprin is described in terms that remind us of those infantile dogmatics about the cat and the mat, and 'run, fox, run': 'He soars and he sinks ... He is holy and he is coarse; he is sublime and he is flat.'

Between this introduction and the preface contributed by the translator, Mr Pasvolsky, who is at naive pains to inform us when Kuprin is at his best, and why he is at his best, the author makes a difficult bow. But happily the first story, which gives the title to the book, is wonderfully successful, and so the bow is a triumphant one. 'The Garnet Bracelet' is a story of hopeless love. It tells how a poor official fell in love with the beautiful Princess Vera Nicolaeyna. For seven years he wrote to her, and then on her birthday he sent her the bracelet. At this her husband and brother interfered. They sought the man out, and he, after giving them to understand that he fully realized the impossibility of the situation, promised them to disappear. Next day the Princess read of his suicide. She received from him a letter written just before he had shot himself, expressing his happiness in having loved her, and begging her to ask someone to play for her, in his memory, the Largo Appassionata from Sonata 2, Op. 2, of Beethoven. From this old-fashioned plot, old-fashioned like the poor bracelet with its ill-polished stones, the green stone in the middle with the five deep red ones surrounding, there come rays of deep quivering light, and all that they reveal is linked together just for one moment, becomes part of the tragic life-story of the strangely simple man for whom 'to love was enough'. 'May nothing transient or vain trouble your beautiful soul!' he writes. But the life of the Princess is composed of what is transient and vain; the society in which he lives is transient and vain; real love could have no part in it. But being a woman her secret dream is of a love that shall fill her whole life; it has come near her, and now it is gone for ever.

The other stories in the book do not approach the first. 'Horse Thieves' and 'The Jewess' are, we imagine, written under the influence of Tchehov. The first, which is an account of a little boy's association with beggars and thieves, and contains a hideous picture of mob violence, has many a touch which puts us in mind of the great writer, but only to marvel, before Kuprin's heaviness, at the delicacy and surety of the other. In 'The Jewess', again, it is easy to see in what soil the idea has been nourished. But a sorry weed has grown, coarse, straggling, with no flower at all for all the author's urging, until at the last he has propped it up with an old stick of allegory which never for an instant deceives us.

A word must be said about 'An Evening Guest'. In a letter giving a list of the works he considers his most successful the author places it first. This is very interesting, as showing the extraordinary difference between the Russian consciousness and ours. To us 'The Evening Guest' is quite impossible; it is very nearly absurd in its ingenuousness. One evening somebody knocks at the writer's door. It sets him wondering who is there, who might be there, and how unknown is the future. He compares life at great length to a game of cards, and then imagines that some madman should hit upon the idea of a lottery of life. On an appointed day there would stand an enormous urn filled with cards, one of which we must draw. And then what is life except this drawing of lots out of an urn of fate? And so on until he falls to wondering whether he will be able to make certain sounds to which the other person on the other side of the door will respond. Until finally, when we are almost inclined to call it childish, he cries, 'Every time that I think of the vastness, complexity, darkness, and elemental accidentality of this general intertwining of lives, my own life appears to me like a tiny speck of dust tossed in the fury of a tempest.' What more is to be said?

Review of Growth of the Soil *by Knut Hamsun*[36]
('A Norwegian Novel', 11 June 1920; in full)

It is difficult to account for the fact that *Growth of the Soil*, the latest novel by the famous Norwegian writer, is only the second of his works to be translated into English. Knut Hamsun is no longer young; he has fulfilled his early promise and his reputation is assured and yet, except for *Shallow Soil*, which was published some years ago, we have had nothing but the echo of his fame to feed upon. Perhaps this is not wholly lamentable. How often we find ourselves wishing that we had the books of some writer we treasure to read for the first time, and if the novel before us is typical of Knut Hamsun's work – as we have every reason to believe it is – there is a feast before us. Here, at least, are four hundred and six pages of small type excellently translated, upon which we congratulate the Norwegian publishers and the translator, whose name does not appear.

If *Growth of the Soil* can be said to have any plot at all – any story – it is the very ancient one of man's attempt to live in fellowship with Nature. It is a trite saying when we are faced with a book which does renew for us the wonder and the thrill of that attempt that never was there a time when its message was more needed. But solitude is no cure for sorrow, and virgin country will not make anyone forget the desolation he has seen. Such a life is only possible for a man like the hero, Isak, a man who has known no other and can imagine none. Nevertheless, there remains in the hearts of nearly all of us an infinite delight in reading of how the track was made, the bush felled, the log hut built, so snug and warm with its great chimney and little door, and of how there were animals to be driven to the long pastures, goats and sheep and a red and white cow. In the opening chapter of *Growth of the Soil*, Knut Hamsun gives us the picture of an immense wild landscape, and there is a track running through it, and we spy a man walking towards the north carrying a sack.

> This or that, he comes; the figure of a man in this great solitude. He trudges on; bird and beast are silent all about him; now and again he utters a word or two speaking to himself. 'Eyah – well, well … ' so he speaks to himself. Here and there, where the moors give place to a kindlier spot, an open space in the midst of the forest, he lays down the sack and goes exploring; after a while he returns, heaves the sack on his shoulders again, and trudges on. So through the day, noting time by the sun; night falls, and he throws himself down on the heather, resting on one arm …

The man is Isak. It is extraordinary, how, while we follow him in his search for the land he wants, the author gives us the man. His slowness and simplicity, his immense strength and determination, even his external appearance, short, sturdy, with a red beard sticking out, and a frown that is not anger, are as familiar as if we had known him in our childhood. It is, indeed, very much as though we were allowed to hold him by the hand and go with him everywhere. The place is found; the hut is built, and a woman called Inger comes from over the hills and lives with him. Gradually, but deeply and largely, their life grows and expands. We are taken into it and nothing is allowed to escape us, and just as we accepted Isak so everything seems to fall into place without question. *Growth of the Soil* is one of those few novels in which we seem to escape from ourselves and to take an invisible part. We suddenly find to our joy that we are walking into the book as Alice walked into the looking-glass and the author's country is ours. It is wonderfully rich, satisfying country, and of all those who dwell in it, gathered round the figures of Isak and Inger, there is not one who does not live. At the end Isak is an old man and his life is ebbing, but the

glow, the warmth of the book seems to linger. We feel, as we feel
with all great novels, that nothing is over.

Review of The Later Life, The Twilight of the Souls, Doctor Adriaan
by Louis Couperus, tr. Alexander Teixeira de Mattos
(extracts from 'The Books of the Small Souls', 18 June 1920)

Those of us who are seriously interested in contemporary fiction
cannot afford to disregard these admirably translated novels by the
famous Dutch author. It is stated in an explanatory note that they
can be read independently and separately, but that is, we think, to
miss the peculiar interest of Mr Couperus' achievement. True, the
first book, which was published some years ago and which bears the
covering title of the series *Small Souls*, may be considered as
complete in itself, but it is also the key to these three that follow
after; and although apart from them, it may and it does strike us as
very brilliant, very sensitive and amazingly vivid and fresh, it is only
when we look back upon it and see it in its rightful place in relation
to the others that we recognize the full significance of the qualities
we admire.

We do not know anything in English literature with which to
compare this delicate and profound study of a passionately united
and yet almost equally passionately divided family. Little by little,
by delicate stages, yet without any preliminary explanations or
reserves, we are taken into the very heart of the matter. The
troubling question which would seem to lie so heavy upon the pen
of many a modern writer: 'How much can I afford to take for
granted? How much dare I trust to the imagination of the reader?' is
answered here. We are too often inclined to think it may be solved by
technical accomplishment, but that is not enough; the reason why
Mr Couperus can afford to dismiss the question, to wave it aside and
to take everything for granted, is because of the strength of his
imaginative vision. By that we mean it is impossible in considering
these books not to be conscious of the deep breath the author has
taken; he has had, as it were, a vision of the Van Lowe family, and he
has seen them as souls – small souls – at the mercy of circumstance,
life, fate. He has realized that that which keeps them together, the
deep impulse which unites them through everything, is
apprehension. The real head of the family, the grim, ghostly
shadow whose authority they never question, is Fear. So, as we
speak of the idea underlying a poem, we may say that fear is the idea

underlying these novels. If we listen deeply enough we can hear this unquiet heart of the Van Lowe family throbbing quickly, and it is because it is never for a moment still that the author succeeds in keeping our interest passionately engaged. We are constantly aware of the vision, the idea; it is the secret that he permits us to share with him, and in the end it seems to give way to a deeper secret still. . . .

There is an angle from which we seem to see them as the strangest landscapes, small, low-lying country swept continually by immense storms of wind and rain, with dark menacing clouds for ever pulling over and casting a weighty shadow that lifts and drifts away only to fall again.

Unsigned review of The Cherry Orchard, *16 July 1920*

We will not insult our readers by supposing, as the critics in other journals are forced to suppose, that they do not know *The Cherry Orchard*. We assume that it is as familiar to them as *Hamlet*, and that they know that to see it acted, however inadequately, is to feel that it is one of the most wonderful plays ever written. The lights are put out, the curtain rises, and we are there, invisible, transported without any explanation or preparation, to that place and time. That is the peculiar strangeness of it. In other plays we have the feeling that the author and the actors are allowing for the fact that there is no fourth wall; in *The Cherry Orchard* we feel that more than the fourth wall is removed; the barriers are down between the characters and ourselves – more, the barriers are down between them and their surroundings. All that comes under the author's spell is bathed, is steeped and saturated in an emotional atmosphere which is compact of silvery whiteness, the pale light of very early morning, the chill of frost, and the mingled fatigue and expectancy that breathes in that hollow room where Dunyasha and Lopahin wait for the sound of wheels.

What an amazing idea it is to let the curtain rise upon that homecoming, and to delay the arrival so that we have time to realize the imaginative significance of the ancient house, so soon to be filled again – of the shabby furniture that looks as though it were profoundly asleep; to taste the chill air and to know that, out there, as far as one can see there are white, glittering trees. So that when Dunyasha cries, 'There they are!' we run with her to welcome them; we share the emotion; it is only chance that we don't unbutton somebody's coat or carry a roll of rugs into the room beyond. And because we have been there before, have, in a moment of time, waited all night long, there is a special, thrilling meaning in all that is said, all that is done – the silence of dawn is broken, is set vibrating and quivering by the returned travellers. It is very late. They ought to be in bed.

Yes, all through *The Cherry Orchard* people are up when they ought to be in bed, talking when they ought to be silent, laughing when they ought to be crying, making jokes when they ought to be making contracts. And the critics who have never in their lives left undone any of the things they ought to have done glare and say: 'This is a tragedy', or glare and say: 'This is a comedy', or glare and say: 'This is a bore.' And some of the actors are as bad as the critics. They cannot conceal their horrible feeling of guilt at the unheard-of conduct that a man of genius has imposed upon them.

It is all very sad, and not at all the kind of spectacle which the respectable dramatic justiciars of *The Times* or the *Daily News* should be invited to witness. No wonder our colleague of *The Times* cannot understand why the Art Theatre should have chosen this play to present to a British audience. God forbid that a British family should recognize itself in this mirror, or feel that these creatures from whom the tyranny of the ought has been lifted are of like passions with themselves. And how we sympathize with him when he finds that Leonid, the brother, and Peter, the tutor, 'are frankly bores'! How we envy him! How deeply we realize that if only we could find them boring we should at last belong to that famous bulldog breed that keeps the Empire going and the circulation of *The Times* at boiling-point.

Alas! we are poor little humans, who hate the ought and feel that it numbs some rich, rare fineness in us, who feel that were it lifted we too might suffer a sea-change and of our bones coral be made; and we rejoice that there has been one man in our age who has had the wisdom and the vision to see these things in us. If we could only be as true to ourselves as the people in *The Cherry Orchard* are to themselves, come as near to others as Tchehov came near to them, 'love our stones' with the same passionate sincerity of the moment as Liubov Andreevna loves hers, admit with the same honesty as they do that they feel freer now the incubus of the home they love has gone, speak to a cupboard with the same flow of sentiment as Leonid does to his – why, then we might not please *The Times*, but something might be done with us.

And as with our souls, so with that crystallization of them which is art. Until a play like *The Cherry Orchard*, so intimate, so real, so beautiful, is felt to be as near and dear to a cultivated British audience as it is to a Russian, there is not much to be done with the English drama. Until our critics feel by instinct that it is to make themselves a laughing-stock to the world to speak of *The Cherry Orchard* and *The Skin Game* in one breath – and we speak as respecters of Mr Galsworthy – whatever may be done with the British drama will wither before the stare of polite in-comprehension. Until our English actors feel themselves at home in, as thrilled by and as proud to act in *The Cherry Orchard* as the artists of the Moscow Theatre did in 1904, whatever may be done with the British drama will be stifled at birth. And here lies the hope. A half-dozen of the actors in the Art Theatre production of *The Cherry Orchard* on Monday acted, not perfectly, not consistently, but at times with a real apprehension of their opportunity. They were Miss Edith Evans (Charlotta), Mr Leyton Cancellor (Gaev), Mr Felix Aylmer (Simemov–Pistchik), Mr William Armstrong (Epihodov), Mr Ernest Patterson (Fiers), and to some extent, in what is really the most difficult part of all, Mr Joseph Dodd as Lopahin. When actors can play as well as these did in the greatest and most delicate of all modern plays for a run of only two nights with rehearsals on the same lavish scale, then we can safely say that it is not for the want of actors that the British drama continues to languish.

CONTEMPORARY WOMEN WRITERS

Review of Heritage *by V. Sackville West*
(extracts from 'A Novel without a Crisis', 30 May 1919)

On page 3 of her novel Miss Sackville West makes an interesting comment:

> I should like to explain here that those who look for facts and events as the central points of significance in a tale will be disappointed. On the other hand I may fall upon an audience which, like myself, contends that the vitality of human beings is to be judged less by their achievement than by their endeavour, by the force of their emotion rather than by their success.

These are not extraordinary words; but we are inclined to think they contain the reason for the author's failure to make important a book which has many admirable qualities.

If we are not to look for facts and events in a novel – and why should we? – we must be very sure of finding those central points of significance transferred to the endeavours and emotions of the human beings portrayed. For, having decided on the novel form, one cannot lightly throw one's story over the mill without replacing it with another story which is, in its way, obedient to the rules of that discarded one. There must be the same setting out upon a voyage of discovery (but through unknown seas instead of charted waters), the same difficulties and dangers must be encountered, and there must be an ever increasing sense of the greatness of the adventure and an ever more passionate desire to possess and explore the mysterious country. There must be given the crisis when the great final attempt is made which succeeds – or does not succeed. Who shall say?

This crisis, then, is the chief of our 'central points of significance' and the endeavours and the emotions are stages on our journey towards or away from it. For without it, the form of the novel, as we see it, is lost. Without it, how are we to appreciate the importance of one 'spiritual event' rather than another? What is to prevent each being unrelated – complete in itself – if the gradual unfolding in growing, gaining light is not to be followed by one blazing moment? . . .

These are bare outlines, richly filled in by the author, and yet we are not 'carried away'. She has another comment:

> Little of any moment occurs in my story, yet behind it all I am aware of tremendous forces at work which none have rightly understood, neither the actors nor the onlookers.

That is easily said. We have heard it so often of late that we are grown a little suspicious, and almost to believe that these are dangerous words for a writer to use. They are a dark shield in his hand when he ought to carry a bright weapon.

Review of Mary Olivier: A Life *by May Sinclair*[37]
('The New Infancy', 5 September 1919; in full)

There has been discovered, of late, cropping up among our

established trees and flowers a remarkable plant, which, while immensely engaging our attention, has not hitherto attained a size and blooming sufficient to satisfy our desire to comprehend it. Little tight buds, half-open flowers that open no further, a blossom or two more or less out – these the plant has yielded. But here at last, with 'Mary Olivier' Miss May Sinclair has given into our grateful hands a full fine specimen.

Is this, we wonder, turning over its three hundred and sixty-eight pages, to be the novel of the future? And if so, whence has it sprung? Who are its ancestors, its parents, its relations, its distant connections even? But the longer we consider it the more it appears to us as a very orphan of orphans, lying in a basket on the threshold of literature with a note pinned on its chest saying: 'If I am to be taken in and welcomed, then the whole rest of the family must be thrown out of the window.' That they cannot exist together seems to us very plain. For the difference between the new way of writing and the old way is not a difference of degree but of kind. Its aim, as we understand it, is to represent things and persons as separate, as distinct, as apart as possible. Here, if you like, are the animals set up on the floor, the dove so different from the camel, the sheep so much bigger than the tiger. But where is the Ark? And where, even at the back of the mind, is the Flood, that dark mass of tumbling water which must sooner or later receive them, and float them or drown them? The Ark and the Flood belong to the old order, they are gone. In their place we have the author asking with indefatigable curiosity: 'What is the effect on this animal upon me, or this or the other one?'

But if the Flood, the sky, the rainbow, or what Blake beautifully calls the bounding outline, be removed and if, further, no one thing is to be related to another thing, we do not see what is to prevent the whole of mankind turning author. Why should writers exist any longer as a class apart if their task ends with a minute description of a big or a little thing? If this is the be-all and end-all of literature why should not every man, woman and child write an autobiography and so provide reading matter for the ages? It is not difficult. There is no gulf to be bridged, no risk to be taken. If you do not throw your Papa and your Mamma against the heavens before beginning to write about them, his whiskers and her funny little nose will be quite important enough to write about, quite enough, reinforced with the pattern of the drawing-room carpet, the valse of the moment and the cook upstairs taking her hair out of pins to make a whole great book. And as B's papa's whiskers and B's mamma's funny little nose are bound to be different again, and their effect upon B again different – why here is high entertainment forever!

Entertainment. But the great writers of the past have not been 'entertainers'. They have been seekers, explorers, thinkers. It has been their aim to reveal a little of the mystery of life. Can one think for one moment of the mystery of life when one is at the mercy of surface impressions? Can one *think* when one is not only taking part but being snatched at, pulled about, flung here and there, cuffed, kissed, and played with? Is it not the great abiding satisfaction of a work of art that the writer was master of the situation when he wrote it and at the mercy of nothing less mysterious than a greater work of art?

It is too late in the day for this new form, and Miss Sinclair's skilful handling of it serves but to make its failure the more apparent. She has divided her history of Mary Olivier into five periods, infancy, childhood, adolescence, maturity and middle-age, but these divisions are negligible. In the beginning Mary is two, but at the end she is still two – and forty-seven – and so it is throughout. At any moment, whatever her real age may be she is two – or forty-seven – either, both. At two (poor infant staggerer!) the vast barn of impressions opens upon her and life, with a pitchfork, tosses her out Mamma, Papa, Mark, Roddy, Dan, Jenny, Catty, Aunt Charlotte, Uncle Victor, and all the rest of them. At forty-seven, although in the meantime many of them have died and died disgustingly, she is still turning them over and over, still wondering whether any of them did happen to have in one of their ignoble pockets the happiness she has missed in life ... For on page 355 she confesses, to our surprise, that is what she has been wanting all along – happiness. Wanting, perhaps, not seeking, not even longing for, but wanting as a child of two might want its doll or its donkey, running into the room where Papa on his dying bed is being given an emetic, to see if it is on the counterpane, running out to see if it is in the cab that has come to take Aunt Charlotte to the Lunatic Asylum, and then forgetting all about it to stare at 'Blanc-mange going round the table, quivering and shaking and squelching under the spoon.'

Review of Tamarisk Town *by Sheila Kaye-Smith*[38]
(extracts from 'A Landscape with Portraits', 12 September 1919)

Were Miss Kaye-Smith a painter, we should be inclined to say that we do not feel she has yet made up her mind which it is that she wishes most to paint – whether landscapes or portraits. Which is it to be? Landscape – the blocking-in of a big difficult scheme, the effort required to make it appear substantial and convincing, the opportunity it gives her for the bold, sweeping line – it is plain to see how strongly this attracts her. Portraits – there is a glamour upon the human beings she chooses which fascinates her, and which she cannot resist. Why should she not be equally at home with both? What is her new novel *Tamarisk Town* but an attempt to see them in relation to each other? And yet, in retrospect, there is her town severely and even powerfully painted, and there are her portraits, on the same canvas, and yet so out of it, so separate that the onlookers' attention is persistently divided – it flies between the two, and is captured by neither. . . .

Marionettes they are, and marionettes they remain, jigging in a high fierce light that Miss Kaye-Smith would convince us is the fire of passion, until the last puppet-quarrel and the last glimpse of the heroine, 'half under the water, half trailing on the rock ... something which, from the top of the cliff, looked like a dead crimson leaf'. This extreme measure is for love of Monypenny, who, at first, is properly grateful for his freedom. Again he is a man like a town walking, until one day he is filled with the idea that his first love is fattening upon the dead body of his second love, and that, after all, a woman is more to be desired than bricks and mortar. This starts working passion number three – he will kill that which killed her, and so have his revenge.

Here, to our thinking, the book ends. All that is going to happen has happened; we are at the top of the hill. Below us lies Marlingate, in its prosperity, 'lying there licked by the sun', and gazed upon by the man who has made it, and is about to unmake it. But the author is, if we may be pardoned the expression, 'as fresh as when she started'. New characters appear – a wife for Monypenny, a little wooden son who has time to grow up and marry the daughter of Morgan le fay (so like, yet so unlike) and to live his father's history all over again before Marlingate is destroyed. And the years roll by, unbroken, heavy, like waves slapping against the promenade, the vulgar pier, before Miss Kaye-Smith is content to leave Marlingate to its fate.

How does it happen that a writer, obviously in love with writing, is yet not curious? This is the abiding impression left us by Miss Kaye-Smith; she is satisfied to put into the mouths and the hearts and minds of her characters the phrase, the emotion, the thought that 'fits' the situation, with the result that it does not seem to matter whether they speak, feel or think. Nothing is gained by it. They are just what they are. The plot's the thing – and having decided upon it she gets her team together and gives out the parts. There is but to speak them. And into the hand of Morgan le fay she thrusts a scarlet umbrella, she throws a cherry cloak about her and clothes her in a scarlet dress – and sets her going.

Review of Potterism *by Rose Macaulay*[39]
('A Springe to Catch Woodcocks', 4 June 1920; in full)

In this new novel by Miss Macaulay it is not only her cleverness and wit which are disarming. It is her coolness, her confidence, her determination to say just exactly what she intends to say whether the reader will or no. We are conscious, while the dreadful truth escapes us, of a slightly bewildered feeling, of, almost, a sense of pique. After all, what right has the author to adopt this indifferent tone towards us? What is the mystery of her offhand, lightly-smiling manner? But these little, quick, darting fishes of doubt remain far below our surface until we are well into the book; we are conscious of them, and that is all. The rest of us is taken up with the enjoyment of 'Potterism', with the description of the Potter Press and what it stands for. It is extraordinarily pleasant to have all our frantic and gloomy protestations and furies against 'Potterism' gathered up and expressed by Miss Macaulay with such precision and glittering order – it is as though she has taken all those silly stones we have thrown and replaced them with swift little arrows. 'How good that is, how true!' we exclaim at every fresh evidence of Potterism and every fresh source of a Potterite ... But then there is her plot to be taken into account. It is very slight. She has simply traced a ring round the most important, the most defined anti-Potterites and Potterites. Potterism is the strongest power that rules England to-day; the anti-Potterites are that small handful of people, including ourselves, whose every breath defies it. And what happens to them? Here those small fishes begin to grow very active, to flirt their fins, flash to the surface, leap, make bubbles. This creates a strange confusion in our minds. For the life of us we can't for the moment see, when all is said and done, which are which. Is it possible that we ourselves are only another manifestation of the disease? Who has won, after all? Who shall say where Potterism ends? It is easy to cry: 'If we must be flung at anything, let us be flung at lions.' But the very idea of ourselves as being flung is an arch-Potterism into the bargain.

Review of Open the Door *by Catherine Carswell* [40]
(extract from 'A Prize Novel', 25 June 1920)

But when Mrs Carswell's novel has been taken down from its small particular eminence and examined apart we must write more warily. *Open the Door*, which is an extremely long novel – it has four hundred pages, that is about one hundred and eighty thousand words – is an account of the coming of age of a young Scottish girl. By coming of age we mean, in this case, the moment when Life ceases to be master, but, recognizing that the pupil has learned all that is needful, gives her her freedom, that she may, in turn, give it to the man who holds her happiness in his keeping. So, from the age of thirteen to the age of thirty, we find ourselves – how is it best expressed? – in the company of Joanna Bannerman, her family, her friends and her lovers. We are told of the influences that hold back or help to unfold the woman in her; her thoughts, feelings and emotions are described with untiring sympathy and skill: but how much, when all is said and done, do we really know of her? How clearly is she a living creature to our imagination? She is receptive, easily led, fond of the country, especially fond of birds, pools, heather, the seasons and their change, and, since she is almost constantly aware of her physical being, her sexual desires are strong.

> At eighteen, a little weary of fruitless emotion, a little dream-sick, the conviction had begun to force itself on Joanna that she was without attraction. For the past ten years she had lavished unreciprocated passion on individuals of both sexes ...

This persistent and deliberate search is perhaps peculiar to a certain character; but for the rest might not Joanna be anybody? We look in vain for the key to her – for that precious insight which sets her apart from the other characters and justifies their unimportance. The family group, for instance, is solidly stated, yet it is conveyed to us that of them all Joanna was the only one that really mattered, because she was the one that broke away. But we never felt her truly bound. And then the men – are they not the shadows of shadows?

There is young Bob, who cries when he ought to have kissed her; her sensational Italian husband breathing fire, Pender, the man of the world, and in the background Lawrence, who without her 'conceived of his life as a seed foiled of its consummation'. They are men only in so far as they are male to Joanna female.

All would be well, in fact, if the author did not see her heroine plus, and we did not see her minus. We cannot help imagining how interesting this book might have been if, instead of glorifying Joanna, there had been suggested the strange emptiness, the shallowness under so great an appearance of depth, her lack of resisting power which masquerades as her love of adventure, her power of being at home anywhere because she was at home nowhere. Mrs Carswell has great gifts, but except in her portrait of Joanna's fanatical mother, she does not try them. They carry her away.

Review of A Fool in her Folly *by Rhoda Broughton*[41]
(extracts from 'Victorian Elegance', 20 August 1920)

In the sympathetic short preface which Mrs Belloc Lowndes has written for this, Miss Broughton's last novel, she tells us that Miss Broughton was 'curiously humble about her books. It was almost as if she was content to regard her literary gift as a kind of elegant accomplishment ... ' Why should this astonish Mrs Belloc Lowndes? It is delightful to think that the author should have been so nice a judge of her talent, for that, after reading *A Fool in her Folly*, is precisely what we feel it to have been – 'a kind of elegant accomplishment'. It is far from our desire to be lacking in respect for Miss Broughton's memory; but why does Mrs Lowndes trouble to quote the 'acute modern critic writing for Americans' when he declares that Miss Broughton 'seemed to him the nearest thing [sic] in spirit to Jane Austen that we have had in recent times'?

There can be no question of comparison between them. That Miss Broughton always put the best of herself into everything she did is undoubtedly true, but that she could have, even if she would have, put all of herself into anything that she did is quite a different matter. We do not think she had any such aim. . . .

The tepidity, almost bordering on idiocy, of her family circle, their politeness, forbearance, gentleness and modesty towards one another, are excellently described, as is the scene between her parents and herself when the fatal manuscript is discovered. For her crime, and to save her family from being corrupted by her very presence among them, she is sent away to a widowed Aunt, and there, meeting a real live man, who is as wicked as he is handsome, she learns to live her book over again. This time she is saved by a friend of the Aunt's and sent home – to spend the remainder of her life – i.e. sixty years – repenting. But what had she written? Either it was pestiferous balderdash or it was all nonsense. Either her parents were idiots or she was a little horror. And what happened between her and the villain thus to destroy her whole life? And was her mind a perfect sink or was she merely the victim of growing curiosity? All these questions are left *dans le vague* – in that dreamy, faint, dazed world where girls of thirteen and girls of eighty-five laugh and cry over the same book.

THE WAR

Review of My War Experiences in Two Continents *by S. Macnaughtan (extract from 'Portrait of a Little Lady', 25 April 1919)*

In the beginning of this book there is a portrait of a little lady sitting upright and graceful in a high-backed chair. She wears an old-world, silk brocade gown fastened with a row of little buttons. There is fine lace at the neck, and a delicate scarf slips from her shoulders. As she leans her cheek on two fingers, her intent, unsmiling gaze is very gentle. But her eyes and lips – typical Northern eyes and lips – challenge her air of sheltered leisure. It would be hard to deceive those eyes – they are steady, shrewd and far-seeing; and one feels that the word that issues from those firm determined lips would be her bond.

It is the portrait of Miss Macnaughtan, who gave the last two years of her life, from July 1914 to September 1916, to suffering humanity, and died as the result of the hardships she endured.

There were women whom nobody had ever 'wanted', young women who longed to put their untried strength to the test, women who never kindled except at the sight of helplessness and suffering, vain women whose one desire was to be important, and unimaginative women who craved a sporting adventure – for all of them the war unlocked the gates of life, and they entered in and breathed the richer air and were content at last.

How different was Miss Macnaughtan's case! She was one of those admirable single Englishwomen whose lives seem strangely fulfilled and complete. She had a home she loved, many friends, leisure for her work, a feeling for life that was a passion, and an immense capacity for happiness. But the war came to her, locking the gates of life. 'I think something in me has stood still or died', she confessed.

Except for a few family letters, her experiences in Belgium, North France, Russia, and on the Persian front are written in the form of a diary. But though one feels that her deliberate aim was to set down faithfully what she saw – the result is infinitely more than that. It is a revelation of her inner self which would perhaps never have been revealed in times less terrible and strange. For though her desire for expression was imperative and throughout the book there are signs of the writer's 'literary' longing to register the moment, the glimpse, the scene; it is evident that she had no wish to let her reserved, fastidious personality show through. It happened in spite of her, and there she is for all time, elderly, frail, with her terrible capacity for suffering, her love for humanity, her pride in being 'English', and her burning zeal to sacrifice herself for those who are broken; not because of their weakness, but because they have been strong. Perhaps above all things she loves the Northern courage, not only to endure, but to hide suffering behind a bright shield. But the war makes her cry:

It *isn't right*. This damage to human life is horrible. It is madness to slaughter these thousands of young men. Almost at last, in a rage, one feels inclined to cry out against the sheer imbecility of it. The pain of it is all too much. I am *sick* of seeing suffering.

And:

… Above all, one feels – at least I do – that one is always, and quite palpably, in the shadow of the death of youth – beautiful youth, happy and healthy and free. Always I seem to see the white faces of boys turned up to the sky, and I hear their cries and see the agony which youth was never meant to bear. They are too young for it, far too young; but they lie out on the field … and bite the mud in their frenzy of pain; and they call for their mothers and no one comes … Who can listen to a boy's groans and his shrieks of pain? This is war.

Again:

> A million more men are needed – thus the fools called men talk.
> But youth looks up with haggard eyes, and youth, grown old,
> knows that Death alone is merciful.

As one reads on one becomes more and more aware how unfitted by nature Miss Macnaughtan was for the great part which she accepted and played so magnificently. Nothing short of rude youth could have stood the wet and cold, lack of sleep, horrible food, agonizing discomfort at the little railway station where she chopped up vegetables for soup, journeys that (only to read of) are a torment. But she was always ill; she loathed communal life with its meanness, pettiness, scandal and muddling untidiness. How can people behave like this – at such a time? she seems to cry. And little by little her weariness turns to disgust, and she cannot bear it. She sorrowfully turns aside – all her love goes out to suffering youth. Nothing else matters.

> I wish I could give my life for some boy who would like to live very
> much, and to whom all things are joyous. But alas! one can't swop
> lives like this …

When she writes that, she is dying. Her journal ends with the words:

> I should like to have left the party[42] – quitted the feast of life –
> when all was gay and amusing. I should have been sorry to come
> away, but it would have been far better than being left till all the
> lights are out. I could have said truly to the Giver of the feast,
> 'Thanks for an excellent time.' But now so many of the guests
> have left, and the fires are going out, and I am tired. . . .

> > *I did not say what I set out to say. It is*
> > *not close knit enough. No, it* won't
> > do.

Review of A Man and his Lesson *by W. B. Maxwell*
(extract from 'Dea Ex Machina', 26 September 1919)

But this time there is Mabel, the sanctity of home life, his reputation, the good opinion of London's dramatic critics to be considered; Diana has to use her telephone quite desperately before he is won back. Four days and nights of bliss, and he returns to Mabel and the children a ruined man, determined to take veronal before his disgrace is made known. But in that dark hour the housemaid brings in the *Daily Mail* – and war is declared between England and Germany. Hurrah for August, 1914! He is saved. Off he goes to be honourably killed. Off he goes to the greatest of all garden parties[43] – and this time there is no doubt as to his enjoying himself. War has its black side, but the lessons – the lessons it teaches a man! Where else shall a man learn the value of brotherly love, the wisdom and friendliness of the generals at the Base, the beauty of Mr Lloyd George's phrase 'the War to end war', the solid worth and charm of a London restaurant, a London club, a London theatre? Diana died while the garden party was at its liveliest, and Vaile was thus freed to live, to be wounded, to confess his fault to Mabel, and to be forgiven. So, after having 'come out again to the grand old task', to 'strike another blow for England and the cause', Bryan Vaile is free to go home, having learned his last and greatest lesson, which is never to answer the telephone again.

THE SHORT-STORY FORM

Review of The Mills of the Gods *by Elizabeth Robins*[44]
(extract from 'Wanted, a New World', 25 June 1920)

Suppose we put it in the form of a riddle: 'I am neither a short story, nor a sketch, nor an impression, nor a tale. I am written in prose. I am a great deal shorter than a novel; I may be only one page long, but, on the other hand, there is no reason why I should not be thirty. I have a special quality – a something, a something which is immediately, perfectly recognizable. It belongs to me; it is of my essence. In fact I am often given away in the first sentence. I seem almost to stand or fall by it. It is to me what the first phrase of the song is to the singer. Those who know me feel: 'Yes, that is it.' And they are from that moment prepared for what is to follow. Here are, for instance, some examples of me: 'A Trifle from Life', 'About Love', 'The Lady with the Dog'. What am I?

It does not appear from *The Mills of the Gods*, however, that the question has ever troubled Miss Elizabeth Robins. The seven tales in this new volume are of a kind that might have appeared in any successful high-class magazine. They are wholesome, sentimental, and not so inconveniently thrilling that the train carries you past your station. Experience, confidence, and a workmanlike style – the author has all three, and they go far to disguise the hollowness beneath the surface, but the hollowness is there. There is not one of the seven which will stand examination. How is it that the author can bear to waste her time over these false situations which are not even novel? How can she bear to put her pen to describing the great-hearted, fearless, rude, swearing, murdering toughs who frequent the Golden Sand Gambling Hell at Nome? those types whom we know as if they had been our brothers, whose hats are off at the word 'Mother', and who shoot the cook who denies them a can of peaches. And then to add to them a little golden-haired innocent child whose father dies, and whom they adopt and send to Europe to finish her studies, and write to in their huge childish fists, telling her she is never to go out without her chaperone and they all send their love! Oh, Miss Robins! We are very, very weary of this kind of tale, and if we cannot refrain from smiling at the love story of the passionate Italian whom 'his intimates in Italy and elsewhere' called Satanucchio, it is not because we are amused.[45]

THE PAST, AND WRITING AS A COLONIAL

Review of The Gay-Dombeys *by Sir Harry Johnston*
(extract from 'A Victorian Jungle', 2 May 1919)

It is not without a tinge of malicious satisfaction that we realize there are delights reserved for us elderly creatures which are quite out of sight, out of reach, of the golden boys and girls who are making so wonderfully free of our apples and pears and plums. Perhaps one of the rarest and most delicious is meeting with an old play-fellow who is just come from the country of our childhood, and having an endless talk with him about what is changed and what is the same – whether the Allens still live in the same house, what has become of the huge Molesworth family, and was the mystery of old Anderson ever solved.[46]

We shall never see these people again; we shall share nothing more with them. We shall never push open their garden gates and smell our way past the flower bushes to the white verandahs where they sit gossiping in the velvet moonlight. Why should we feel then this passionate interest? Is it because, prisoners as we are, we love to feel we have inhabited other lives – lived more lives than one – or we are reluctant to withdraw wholly because of that whispered word 'Finis' which locks the doors against us, one by one, for ever?

The memory of our childhood is like 'the memory of a tale that is told', and the delight of talking over with a boon companion a book you have read in the long ago is hardly less real. It is very different; you are both left wondering. What happened 'after that'? Does the author know? Or does he – wonder too? What would Dickens say if he read Sir Harry Johnston's *Gay-Dombeys*, which continues the history of the Dombey family and their circle through the Victorian period and into our own times, with wonderful elaborateness and excursions and allusions such as their author loved, and with a canvas so crowded that you have to stand on tiptoe and look over people's shoulders and under their arms and round them before you can be perfectly sure that you have seen everybody who is there?

We can think of no other author who took a final farewell of his characters with greater reluctance than did Dickens. His meanest villains were, after all, citizens of his world, and as such they stumbled and were up again, to be nearly caught, and again escaped before he could bear to let them go for ever. As to those whom he loved – and in whom he lived – it was anguish to him to submit to their passing. 'Shall I never be that dying boy again, waving my hand at the water on the wall? Never be again the child-wife Little Blossom, asking if my poor boy is very lonely downstairs?' And so the boat puts back once more for one last sob, one last gush of tears. Even the survivors were not allowed to gather without one final Grand Tableau before the fall of the curtain, which is intended for an abiding proof for him and for us that they are still there, still going on, still extravagantly, abundantly alive. . . .

> *Nothing like good enough. Too big an*
> *avenue; practically* no *house at the*
> *end of it – at any rate no solid house*
> *and no firm hold. Very very bad.*

Review of The Story of a New Zealand River *by Jane Mander*
(extract from 'First Novels', 9 July 1920)

The case of Miss Jane Mander is very different. Her *Story of a New*

Zealand River, which takes four hundred and thirty-two pages of small type to tell, has none of Miss Symonds' sophistication, or European atmosphere.[47] The scene is laid in the back blocks of New Zealand, and, as is almost invariably the case with novels that have a colonial setting, in spite of the fact that there is frequent allusion to the magnificent scenery, it profiteth us nothing. 'Stiff laurel-like puriris stood beside the drooping lace fringe of the lacy rimu; hard blackish kahikateas brooded over the oak-like ti-toki with its lovely scarlet berry.' What picture can that possibly convey to an English reader? What emotion can it produce? But that brings us to the fact that Miss Jane Mander is immensely hampered in her writing by her adherence to the old unnecessary technical devices – they are no more – with which she imagines it necessary to support her story. If one has the patience to persevere with her novel, there is, under all the false wrappings, the root of something very fresh and sturdy. She lacks confidence and the courage of her opinions; like the wavering, fearful heroine, she leans too hard on England. There are moments when we catch a bewilderingly vivid glimpse of what she really felt and knew about the small settlement of people in the lumber-camp, but we suspect that these are moments when she is off her guard. Then her real talent flashes out; her characters move quickly, almost violently; we are suddenly conscious what an agony, what an anguish it was to Bruce when he felt one of his drunken fits coming on; or The Boss reveals his extraordinary simplicity when he tells his wife he thought she'd been unfaithful to him for years.

But these serve nothing but to increase our impatience with Miss Mander. Why is her book not half as long, twice as honest? What right has she to bore her readers if she is capable of interesting them? It would be easy to toss *The Story of a New Zealand River* aside and to treat it as another unsuccessful novel, but we have been seeking for pearls in such a prodigious number of new books that we are forced to the conclusion that it is useless to dismiss any that contain something that might one day turn into a pearl. What is extremely impressive to the novel reviewer is the modesty of the writers – their diffidence in declaring themselves what they are – their almost painful belief that they must model themselves on somebody. We turn over page after page wondering numbly why this unknown he or she should go through the labour of writing all this down. They cannot all of them imagine that this book is going to bring them fame and fortune. And then – no, not always, but a great deal more often than the cultivated public would believe – there is a sentence, there is a paragraph, a whole page or two, which starts in the mind of the reviewer the thrilling thought that this book was written because the author wanted to write. How is this timidity to be explained, then? One would imagine that round the corner there was a little band of jeering, sneering, superior persons ready to leap up and laugh if the cut of the new-comer's jacket is not of the strangeness they consider admissible. In the name of the new novel, the new sketch, the new story, if they are really there, let us defy them.

THE 'PASTIME' NOVEL

Review of Crabtree House *by Howel Evans*
('Anodyne', 25 July 1919; in full)

What is a 'sweetly pretty' novel? Standing in the library waiting for the book which never is in, we are constantly hearing this term of recommendation used by a certain type of young lady. 'Oh, do read *Room for Two*. Of course *The Fireplace* is interesting and awfully thrilling and exciting, but it is not sweetly pretty.' And the sweetly pretty book wins the day.

We imagine it is a novel which sets out to prove that the only form of government is government by the heart alone, and for the heart alone. There is a dreadful black monster, a kind of wild bull, looking over the fence at the innocent undefended picnic and plotting and planning how he may come in and upset and trample all – it is the mind. Beware of it. Have nothing to do with it. Shun it as you would your mortal enemy. The innocent, the simple, the loyal, the trusty, the faithful, the uncomplaining – all, all are children of the heart. Have they ever plotted and planned, ever lain tossing through the dark hours – and thinking; ever smiled strangely and disappeared; ever slunk down narrow streets muttering something and frowning? Never! These are the habits of villains, of schemers, adventurers and clever men – these are the signs by which ye may know the children of the mind. If the mind triumphs – where is your happy ending? And as we understand the sweetly pretty novel it is part of its 'appeal' that you are never out of sight of the happy ending from the very first page. Your faith is tried, but not unduly tried; the boat may rock a little and a dash or two of spray come over, but you are never out of harbour – never so much as turned towards the open sea.

Poor little human beings! from the success of the sweetly pretty novel one may learn how difficult it is for them to keep their faith intact in the triumph of good over evil. What consolation to turn from the every-day world with its obscure processes and its happy endings so remarkably well hidden to another existence where every other moment they may have the comfort of crying: 'There now! I knew that was going to happen!'

What the outside reader does feel inclined to question is whether the simple people need be so incredibly simple and the innocent characters innocent to imbecility.

The heroine of *Crabtree House*, for instance, at the age of nineteen when about to tell her father that her young man wishes to marry her, goes to these lengths:

> ' ... and Dad – ' Rosie came up and fingered her father's collar, and put his tie straight and whispered a little shyly: 'he – he – he's been asking me when – when it's to be. You know what I mean, Dad, don't you? And I said, well, that – he – I – he – we must ask you, Dad. Don't you see?'

That is hard enough to bear. But when Rose delivers herself later of:

> 'But there, I won't speak any more of that, Daddy ... I know it only makes you sad, and Daddie – may I – may I, to-night, like I used to when I was a little girl, and you used to call me Goldilocks, may I say my prayers on your knees?'
>
> Amos could only smooth that silken hair once more; he could not trust himself to answer; and Rosie knelt at her father's knees and with eyes shut and hands folded prayed in silence ...

we seem to hear the 'Broken Melody' as we read and the waves beating against the Eastbourne Pier. Let us be grateful to Mr Howel Evans that we are not with Rosie and her husband in the early months of their wedded life when Rosie is caught hemming an infinitesimal garment ...

But apart from this embarrassing exaggeration of the characters' heavenly qualities *Crabtree House* is as nice an example of the sweetly pretty novel as you might wish to find. Heart and mind are nicely balanced against each other, and though you would not doubt the

issue of the fight, you cannot be absolutely certain how the victory
will be obtained, and so – you read on.

Review of The Ancient Allan *by H. Rider Haggard*
(extract from 'Mystery and Adventure', 27 February 1920)

The Ancient Allen, Sir Rider Haggard's new novel, is a far simpler
variety of the pastime novel. It opens on a familiar note:

> Now I, Allan Quatermain, come to the weirdest (with one or two
> exceptions perhaps) of all the experiences which it has amused me
> to employ my idle hours in recording here in a strange land, for
> after all England is strange to me.

This is the kind of thing to settle down to when the destination is
Devonshire, if it is not Cornwall; but, alas! it needs – it dreadfully
needs – the flying interruptions outside the carriage window – the
mysterious interruptions of people's sandwiches – the indignant
emotion aroused by the tea-basket, and the blissful sight of the train
making a great scallop round the blue edge of the sea – to enable us
to swallow such a very dusty dose of ancient Egypt.
    Here is battle, murder and sudden death, wheels within chariot
wheels, villains and heroes and black slaves, who in their land were
kings; here is the mighty battle with the crocodile, the torture of the
boat – all the ingredients that once upon a time, only to get a whiff
of, knew us hungry. But nowadays to read of how one was placed in
an open boat and another boat put on top, so that only the heads and
hands remained outside – to be launched on a river and allowed to
linger – awakes no response in us at all.

Review of The Captives *by Hugh Walpole*
('Observation Only', 15 October 1920; in full)

If an infinite capacity for taking pains were what is needed to
produce a great novel, we should have to hail Mr Walpole's latest
book as a masterpiece. But here it is – four parts, four hundred and
seventy pages, packed as tight as they can hold with an assortment of
strange creatures and furnishings; and we cannot, with the best will
in the world, see in the result more than a task – faithfully and
conscientiously performed to the best of the author's power – but a

'task accomplished', and not even successfully at that. For we feel that it is determination rather than inspiration, strength of will rather than the artist's compulsion, which has produced *The Captives*. Still, while we honour the author for these qualities, is it not a lamentable fact that they can render him so little assistance at the last – can give him no hand with this whole great group of horses captured at such a cost of time and labour, and brought down to the mysterious water only that they shall drink? But, alas! they will not drink for Mr Walpole; he has not the magic word for them; he is not their master. In a word, for all his devotion to writing, we think the critic, after an examination of *The Captives*, would find it hard to state with any conviction that Mr Walpole is a creative artist. These are hard words; we shall endeavour to justify our use of them.

But first let us try to see what it is that Mr Walpole has intended to 'express' in his novel – what is its central idea. 'If this life be not a real fight in which something is eternally gained for the universe by success … ' It is, we imagine, contained in these words of William James. A *real* fight – that is the heart of the matter – and waged in this life and for this life that something may be eternally gained. Maggie Cardinal, a simple, ardent creature with a passion to live, to be free, to be herself and of this world, is caught as she steps over the threshold of her Aunt Anne's house in a burning, fiery trap. Maggie is, we are told over and over, a child of nature, ignorant, simple, rough, but with a loving heart. She has a persistent feeling, however, that she is different from all the rest of the world, and that she will never belong to anyone. Her nineteen years of life have been spent in the wilds with a disreputable father. But at his death she is captured by her Aunt Anne and by the fanatic religious sect to which her Aunt belongs. The head of the Kingscote Brethren is Mr Warlock, and Martin, his son, is the second captive. Maggie's father and Maggie's aunt are determined, with all the passion of their fanatic souls, to offer these two to God when he descends, as they believe he may do at any moment, in his chariot of fire. Hence their cry, torn from them, to be free – to be allowed to fight in this world; hence their struggle. But when, after endless complications and separations, they are released from their fiery bonds, what happens? What has been the significance of all this to them? We are led to believe that both of them are conscious, while they are fighting the world of Aunt Anne and Mr Warlock, that, nevertheless, they do acknowledge the power of some mysterious force outside themselves – which may … some day … what? We are

left absolutely in the air. Maggie and Martin, together at last –
Martin, a broken man, and Maggie happy because somebody needs
her – are not living beings at the end any more than they are at the
beginning; they will not, when Mr Walpole's pen is lifted, exist for a
moment.

But apart from the author's failure to realize his idea, the working
out of *The Captives* is most curiously superficial. Mr Walpole acts as
our guide to these strange people, but what does he know of them?
We cannot remember a novel where we were more conscious of the
author's presence on every page; but he is there as a stranger, as an
observer, as someone outside it all. How hard he tries – how
painfully he fails! His method is simply to amass observations – to
crowd and crowd his book with figures, scenes, bizarre and fantastic
environments, queer people, oddities. But we feel that no one
observation is nearer the truth than another. For example, take his
description of Aunt Anne's house. The hall, we are told, smelt of
'damp and geraniums', on another occasion of 'damp biscuits and
wet umbrellas', on another of 'cracknel biscuits and lamp oil'. What
did it smell of? And how many times is hissing gas mentioned to
make our blood creep? The disquiet pursues us even to the sordid
lodgings in King's Cross, where the hall is lighted by a flickering
candle, and yet Maggie, in the filthy little sitting-room *presses the bell*
for the servant-maid. But above all let us take Maggie. She has read
practically nothing – 'that masterpiece, *Alice in Wonderland*', and
'that masterpiece, *Robinson Crusoe*', '*The Mysteries of Udolpho*', and
certain other books. But 'the child (for she was nothing more)', as
the author countless times assures us, was totally ignorant. Yet
entering her aunt's drawing-room for the first time, and stumbling:
'They'll think me an idiot who can't enter a room properly', she
reflects. This is a highly sophisticated reflection, surely. And she
takes a taxi, pays a call, knows just how to address the London maid
at the door – behaves, in fact, like a perfect lady. Yet 'it is a sufficient
witness to Maggie's youth and inexperience' that she is startled and
amazed by a cuckoo clock. She did not know such things existed!
Again, would that girl notice how much stronger and firmer her
uncle's thighs looked when he came to see her in London – would
she notice too, at a moment of dreadful stress, the size and
plumpness of her husband's thighs 'pressing out against the shiny
black cloth of his trousers'? Are these *her* observations? No, they are
the literary observations of the author. And above all, is it possible
that the greenest of young persons would trust the gay, saucy Miss

Caroline Smith? In describing Maggie's relation to Caroline, Mr Walpole appears to have relied on Dickens for his female psychology and his manner; but Dickens is a false friend to his heroine. And who could have taught Aunt Anne's parrot 'Her golden hair was hanging down her back'? And why should Mr Warlock, in the aunt's drawing-room, ask Maggie to 'forgive' his speaking to her – as though they had met at a pillar-box? And who can accept her marriage with the Reverend Paul, in the 'shadow of whose heart' – for all her physical horror of him – she 'fell into deep, dreamless slumber'?

Thus do we receive shock after minute shock, each one leaving us chillier. But in spite of it all, the feeling that remains is the liveliest possible regret that Mr Walpole should have misjudged his powers – so bravely.

Compare the following letters. In the first, to Murry, KM emphasises the importance of this particular review, and in the second, to Walpole, she expands – gently – on what she had to say in her review.

Walpole's novel which I mean to do for next week (1 col) ought to be a very good prop to hang those very ideas on that I have tried to communicate to you.[48] I want to take it seriously and really say why it fails – for, of course, it does fail. But his 'intention' was serious. I hope I'll be able to say what I do mean. I am *no* critic of the homely kind. 'If you would only explain quietly in simple language', as LM said to me yesterday. Good Heavens, that *is* out of my power.

(To J. M. Murry, 4 October 1920)

I must answer your letter immediately. It has dropped into the most heavenly fair morning. I wish instead of writing you were here on the terrace and you'd let me talk of your book which I *far* from detested. What an impression to convey! My trouble is I never have enough space to get going – to say what I mean to say – fully. That's no excuse, really. But to be called very unfair – that hurts, awfully, and I feel that by saying so you mean I'm not as honest as I might be. I'm prejudiced. Well, I think we're all of us more or less prejudiced, but cross my heart I don't take reviewing lightly and if I appear to it's the fault of my unfortunate manner.

Now I shall be *dead frank*. And please don't answer. As one writer to another (tho' I'm only a little beginner, and *fully realise* it).

The Captives impressed me as more like a first novel than any genuine first novel I've come across. Of course, there were signs enough that it wasn't one – but the movement of it was the movement of one trying his wings, finding out how they would bear him, how far he could afford to trust them, that you were continually risking yourself, that you had, for the first time, really committed yourself in a book. I wonder if this will seem to you extravagant impertinence. I honoured you for it. You seemed to me determined to shirk nothing. You know that strange sense of insecurity *at the last*, the feeling 'I know all this. I know more. I know down to the minutest detail and *perhaps more still*, but shall I dare to trust myself to tell all?' It is really why we write, as I see it, that we may arrive at this moment and yet – it is stepping into the air to yield to it – a kind of anguish and rapture. I felt that you appreciated this, and that, seen in this light, your *Captives* was almost a spiritual exercise in this kind of courage. But in fact your peculiar persistent consciousness of what you wanted to do was what seemed to me to prevent your book from being a creation. That is what I meant when I used the clumsy word 'task'; perhaps 'experiment' was nearer my meaning. You seemed to lose in passion what you gained in sincerity and therefore 'the miracle' didn't happen. I mean the moment when the act of creation takes place – the mysterious change – when you are no longer writing the book, *it* is writing, *it* possesses you. Does that sound hopelessly vague?

But there it is. After reading *The Captives* I laid it down thinking: Having 'broken with his past' as he has in this book, having 'declared himself', I feel that Hugh Walpole's next novel will be the one to look for. Yes, curse me. I should have said it!

I sympathise more than I can say with your desire to escape from autobiography. Don't you feel that what English writers lack to-day is experience of Life. I don't mean that superficially. But they are self-imprisoned. I think there is a very profound distinction between any kind of *confession* and creative work – not that that rules out the first by any means.   (To Hugh Walpole, 27 October 1920)

Review of The Countess of Lowndes Square; and Other Stories *by E. F. Benson;* Just Open *by W. Pett Ridge;* A Man of the Islands, *by H. de Vere Stacpoole*
(extracts from 'A Set of Four', 26 November 1920)

Mr Benson is a writer to whom, one imagines, everything comes in useful. He is a collector of scraps, snippets, patches, tid-bits, oddments, which give him such a great deal of pleasure that it is with the utmost confidence he displays his little collection to all the other guests in this immense rambling, very noisy and overcrowded hotel. He knows himself to be – his behaviour is that of – a favourite guest. 'Mr E. F. Benson is so popular – so entertaining.' And so in his easy, effortless way out comes another book. Here, he even explains, you've got cats, cranks, spiritualist séances, blackmailers – choose whichever you like; there's something for everybody. So down drops the knitting; the cards are put away; the picture paper is concealed behind a cushion for another time, and *The Countess of Lowndes Square* is no doubt discovered to be *just* like Mr Benson – *most* entertaining this time.

Reader! We are the forlorn guest on these occasions. We are that strange-looking person over in the corner who seems so out of everything and never will mix properly. Spare your knitting-needle; put up your paper-knife, sir. Do not stab us. It is not our fault that we look grim. It isn't pleasant to be bored. Will you believe us when we say we love smiling, we love to be amused? We always think, until faced by these occasions, that it takes too little to make us smile. But there is an atmosphere of bright chatter, of quick, animated glare which is warm South to Mr Benson and his admirers while it freezes our risible folds.

> ... I had been asked by telephone just at luncheon-time as I was sitting down to a tough and mournful omelette alone, and I naturally felt quite certain that I had been bidden to take the place of some guest.

Or listen to the 'adorable Agnes Lockett';

> ... If Mrs Withers had told me any more of what the great ones of the earth said to her in confidence, I should either have gone mad or taken up a handful of those soft chocolates and rubbed her face with them.

But it is perhaps hardly fair to take to pieces what the author himself calls 'digestible snacks'. This, we venture to suggest, should have been the title of the volume. And would it not be an admirable idea if there were a covering title for stories of the author's own description? 'Snacks' for instance, could hardly be improved upon.

'Digestible Snacks' is illuminating; it tells us exactly what we are buying.

We speak thus openly, for Mr Benson confesses that in his opinion 'the short story is not a lyre on which English writers thrum with the firm delicacy of the French, or with the industry of the American author'. He opines that if the ten best short stories in the world were proclaimed they would be French stories; while if the million worst were brought together, they would be found to be written in America. *Chi lo sa!* as d'Annunzio's heroines were so fond of murmuring. But our eye wanders to the small green volumes of Turgeniev and Tchehov. Russia is evidently torn out of Mr Benson's atlas. . . .

Just Open, by Mr Pett Ridge, is adapted for a railway journey on which the train stops at all the stations – one of those journeys when one is constantly rearranging one's knees, saying one does not mind at all having the golf-clubs thrown on to one's paper of violets, and swearing that it is not – and never was, thank God! – one's copy of *The Daily Mirror* on the floor. In these surroundings dips are all the reader is fit for, and dips are all that the author provides – they are sketches of little people who, entangled for ever in the net of circumstance, are yet alive enough to make some protest when they feel an extra jerk. There is a slight commotion, a swimming together, a lashing of tails, a wriggle or two. But it lasts only a minute; with the turn of the blank page there is calm ...

The old theatrical star is tempted to go to see the show one night, and she is recognized and taken behind the scenes and made much of. Again she lifts the glass to her lips, but there is no wine. Just a breath, a sweetness – a memory that she sips – and then all is over. Well – mightn't that be a marvellous story? Isn't it one of the stories that we all keep, unwritten, to write some day, when we have realized more fully that moment, perhaps, when she steps out of the theatre into the cold indifferent dark, or perhaps that moment when the light breaks along the edge of the curtain and the music sinks down, lower, lower, until the fiddles are sounding from under the sea? ... But Mr Pett Ridge gives us his version of it as though he expected it to be read between nine forty-five and ten-thirteen.

'Poor old soul!' we presume his admiring reader thinks, slapping her book together and asking her neighbour if he would mind *not* sitting on her coat any longer as this is her station and she can't afford to jump bodily out of her coat on to the platform? But is that tribute enough? Does that content the author? We wonder because there are 'hints' in several stories that lead us to believe he could, if he would, tell it all so differently.

Mr de Vere Stacpoole, to judge by *A Man of the Islands*, still believes he has only to shake a coral island at us to set us leaping. But we have cut our teeth on it so dreadfully often. We have counted the cocoanuts, discovered the square bottle half-buried in the deserted beach, and fished the lagoon of its last false pearl. The only episode that arrested our attention in this book was when Sigurdson saw the front end of Pilcher down on the coral, scrabbling along on its hands like a crab.

> He'd been bitten off below the waist by a shark that had took him just as a child takes a piece of candy and bites it in two!

What a degradation is this when nothing less fearful will draw us to the ship's side! As to that slender dark girl with the scarlet hibiscus flower behind her ear and her hand lifted in the familiar 'Come to Motuaro' gesture – she makes us almost inclined to signal 'full steam ahead' for the opposite direction. It is not enough to know that the fate of that great, strong man lay in those small, scented hands. What did he feel about it? Did he feel anything? Did they talk together? What did they share? How was his love for her different from his love for a white girl? … Or, if the question is all of the scenery, let us feel the strangeness of it. Sigurdson is a Dane. Did he have more of the feelings of an exile? Here, indeed, is our whole point about coral islands, dark blue seas and crescent beaches pale as the new moon. We will not be put off with pictures any longer. We ask that someone should discover the deeper strangeness for us, so that our imagination is not allowed to go starving while our senses are feasted.

Compare the following letter[49] to Sydney and Violet Schiff (1 December 1920):

I'm *tired* of extinguishing Benson, especially as he shines as bright as ever the moment after. Plague take these books. If it wasn't a question of money – what wouldn't I give to leave them alone and only do my own book. It's an awful wrench to turn from one's work and take up Stacpole [*sic*] or Pett Ridge (what names the fellows have, too!) However – Squire has taken my last long story for the *Mercury*.[50] I don't know when it will appear. It's a study of a man and a woman – People won't like it.

3 Work in Progress: Notes on Writing, 1921–2

In December 1920 KM had written to Murry to say that 'KM couldn't go on' with the *Athenaeum* reviewing. After a stay in Menton in the first part of 1921, she had the most productive period of her writing-career when she was living at Sierre in Switzerland over the summer and autumn of 1921. It was at this time that 'At the Bay', 'The Voyage', 'The Garden Party' and 'The Doll's House' were written. Yet KM remained a stringent critic of her own work: her comments during this period on stories which 'failed' are extremely revealing of her aims and techniques.

Bliss and Other Stories had 'made' KM in 1920, and her *Athenaeum* reviews only added to her reputation. By the time *The Garden Party and Other Stories* was published in February 1922 she had become famous, yet her tactful and acute letters to younger artists display no consciousness of this. Her irritation over much of the dull fiction she undertook to review for the *Daily News* is however made plain in a letter to Sydney and Violet Schiff cited here. These reviews were usually, it seems, unsigned, but an important signed review of Galsworthy's *To Let* is here reprinted for the first time.

I EXTRACTS FROM LETTERS AND JOURNALS

To Richard Murry, [1] *17 January 1921*

It's a very queer thing how *craft* comes into writing. I mean down to details. Par exemple. In 'Miss Brill' I choose not only the length of every sentence, but even the sound of every sentence. I choose the rise and fall of every paragraph to fit her, and to fit her on that day at that very moment. After I'd written it I read it aloud – numbers of times – just as one would *play over* a musical composition – trying to get it nearer and nearer to the expression of Miss Brill – until it fitted her.

Don't think I'm vain about the little sketch. It's only the method I

113

wanted to explain. I often wonder whether other writers do the same – If a thing has really come off it seems to me there mustn't be one single word out of place, or one word that could be taken out. That's how I AIM at writing. It will take some time to get anywhere near there.

But you know, Richard, I was only thinking last night people have hardly begun to write yet. Put poetry out of it for a moment and leave out Shakespeare – now I mean prose. Take the very best of it. Aren't they still cutting up sections rather than tackling the whole of a mind? I had a moment of absolute terror in the night. I suddenly thought of *a living mind* – a whole mind – with absolutely nothing left out. With *all* that one knows how much does one not know? I used to fancy one knew all but some kind of mysterious core (or one could). But now I believe just the opposite. The unknown is far, far greater than the known. The known is only a mere shadow. This is a fearful thing and terribly hard to face. But it must be faced.

To J. M. Murry, 25 May 1921

'The great artist is he who exalts difficulty' – do you believe that? And that it's only the slave (using slave in our mystical sense) who pines for freedom.[2] The free man, the artist, seeks to bind himself. No, these notes aren't any good. But I have been finding out more and more how true it is that it's only the difficult thing that is worth doing; it's the difficult thing that one deliberately chooses to do. I don't think Tchehov was as aware of that as he should have been. Some of the stories in *The Horse-Stealers* are – rather a shock.

Journal, July 1921

I finished 'Mr and Mrs Dove'[3] yesterday. I am not altogether pleased with it. It's a little bit made up. It's not inevitable. I mean to imply that those two may not be happy together – that that is the kind of reason for which a young girl marries. But have I done so? I don't think so. Besides, it's not *strong* enough. I want to be nearer – far, far nearer than that. I want to use all my force even when I am taking a fine line. And I have a sneaking notion that I have, at the end, used the Doves *unwarrantably*. *Tu sais ce que je veux dire.* I used them to round off something – didn't I? Is that quite my game? No, it's not. It's not quite the kind of truth I'm after. Now for 'Susannah'. All must be *deeply felt*.

Journal, 23 July 1921

Finished 'An Ideal Family' yesterday. It seems to me better than 'The Doves', but still it's not good enough. I worked at it hard enough, God knows, and yet I didn't get the deepest truth out of the idea, even once. What *is* this feeling? I feel again that this kind of knowledge is too easy for me; it's even a kind of trickery. I know so much more. This looks and smells like a story, but I wouldn't buy it. I don't want to possess it – to live with it. NO. Once I have written two more, I shall tackle something different – a long story: 'At the Bay', *with more difficult relationships. That's the whole problem.*

Journal, September 1921

' "That's how it is, old girl ... Kuzma Ionitch is gone ... He said goodbye to me ... He went and died for no reason ... Now, suppose you had a little colt, and you were own mother to that little colt ... And all at once that same little colt went and died ... You'd be sorry, wouldn't you?"

The little mare munches, listens, and breathes on her master's hands. Iona is carried away and tells her all about it.' (Tchehov: 'Misery'.)

I would see every single French short story up the chimney for this. It's one of the masterpieces of the world.

Journal, October 1921

I wonder why it should be so difficult to be humble. I do not think I am a good writer; I realize my faults better than anyone else could realise them. I know exactly where I fail. And yet, when I have finished a story and before I have begun another, I catch myself *preening* my feathers. It is disheartening. There seems to be some bad old pride in my heart; a root of it that puts out a thick shoot on the slightest provocation ... This interferes very much with work. One can't be calm, clear, good as one must be, while it goes on. I look at the mountains, I try to pray and I think of something *clever*. It's a kind of excitement within one, which shouldn't be there. Calm yourself. Clear yourself. And anything that I write in this mood will be no good; it will be full of *sediment*. If I were well, I would go off by myself somewhere and sit under a tree. One must learn, one must practise, to *forget* oneself. I can't tell the truth about Aunt Anne

unless I am free to enter into her life without selfconsciousness. Oh
God! I am divided still.

To Dorothy Brett, 11 November 1921

For I put my all into that story ['The Daughters of the Late Colonel']
and hardly anyone saw what I was getting at. Even dear old Hardy
told me to write more about those sisters. As if there was any more
to say! . . .

Tchehov *said* over and over again, he protested, he begged, that
he had no problem.[4] In fact, you know, he thought it was his
weakness as an artist. It worried him, but he always said the same.
No problem. And when you come to think of it, what was Chaucer's
problem or Shakespeare's? The 'problem' is the invention of the
19th Century. The artist takes a long look at life. He says softly, 'So
this is what life is, is it?' And he proceeds to express that. All the rest
he leaves. Tolstoi even had no problem. What he had was a
propaganda and he is a great artist in spite of it.

To William Gerhardi,[5] 14 November 1921

[About *Futility*] I congratulate you. It is a living book. What I mean
by that is, it is warm; one can put it down and it goes on
breathing. . . .

I think, perhaps, the best *moment* is at the end; the scene of your
hero's return and his walk with Nina. There you really are
discovered – a *real* writer. There is such feeling, such warmth in
these chapters. Nina's 'whimsical' voice, those kittens, the sofa with
broken springs, the 'speck of soot on your nose' – and then at the
very end the steamer that would not go. I am not quoting these
things at random, for their charm. But because, taken altogether,
they seem to convey to the reader just the 'mood' you wished to
convey. . . .

Only in Ch. xi, in your description of the 'sisters', I think you
falsify the tone; it seems to me, you begin to tell us what we must feel
about them, what the sight of them perched on the chairs and the
sofas really meant, and that's not necessary. One feels they are
being 'shown off' rather than seen. And you seem in that chapter to
be hinting at something, even a state of mind of your hero's, which
puts the reader off the scent a little. . . .

I don't think this book really holds together enough, even

allowing for the title. It ought to be more squeezed and pressed and moulded into shape and wrung out, if you know what I mean ... please remember, I'm speaking 'ideally'.

Journal, November 1921

Vaihinger: *Die Philosophie des Als Ob.*[6] How comes it about that with curiously false ideas we yet reach conclusions that are in harmony with Nature and appeal to us as Truth?

It is by means of, and not in spite of, these logically defective conceptions that we obtain logically valuable results. The fiction of *Force*: when two processes tend to follow each other, to call the property of the first to be followed by the other its 'force', and to measure that 'force' by the magnitude of the result (*e.g.* force of character). In reality we have only succession and co-existence, and the 'force' is something we imagine.

Dogma: absolute and unquestionable truth.

Hypothesis: possible truth (Darwin's doctrine of descent).

Fiction: is impossible but enables us to reach what is relatively truth.

The myths of Plato have passed through these three stages, and passed back again, i.e. they are now regarded as fiction.

Why must thinking and existing be ever on two different planes? Why will the attempt of Hegel to transform subjective processes into objective world-processes not work out? 'It is the special art and object of thinking to attain existence by quite other methods than that of existence itself.' That is to say, reality cannot become the ideal, the dream; and it is not the business of the artist to grind an axe, to try to impose his vision of life upon the existing world. Art is not an attempt of the artist to reconcile existence with his vision; it is an attempt to create his own world *in* this world. That which suggests the subject to the artist is the *unlikeness* to what we accept as reality. We single out – we bring into the light – we put up higher.

Notes on Shakespeare,[7] *late 1921*

'ALL'S WELL THAT ENDS WELL'

The First Lord is worth attending to. One would have thought that his speeches and those of the Second Lord would have been interchangeable; but he is a very definite, quick-cut character. Take, for example, the talk between the two in Act IV Scene III. The Second Lord asks him to let what he is going to tell dwell darkly with him.

First Lord: 'When you have spoken it, 'tis dead, and I am the grave of it.'

And then his comment:

'How mightily sometimes we make us comforts of our losses.'

And this is most excellent:

'The web of our life is of a mingled yarn, good and ill together; our virtues would be proud if our faults whipped them not; and our faults would despair if they were not cherished by our virtues.'

I like the temper of that extremely – and does it not reveal the man? Disillusioned and yet – amused – worldly, and yet he has feeling. But I see him as – quick, full of life, and marvellously at his ease with his company, his surroundings, his own condition, and the whole small, solid earth. He is like a man on shipboard who is inclined to straddle just to show (but not to *show off*) how well his sea-legs serve him …

The Clown – 'a shrewd knave and an unhappy' – comes to tell the Countess of the arrival of Bertram and his soldiers.

'Faith, there's a dozen of 'em, with delicate fine hats, and most courteous feathers, that bow and nod the head at every man.'

In that phrase there is all the charm of soldiers on prancing, jingling, dancing horses. It is a veritable little pageant. With what an air the haughty (and intolerable) Bertram wears his two-pile velvet patch – with what disdain his hand in the white laced French gloves tightens upon the tight rein of his silver charger. Wonderfully sunny, with a little breeze. And the Clown, of course, sees the humour of this conceit …

Parolles is a lovable creature, a brave little cock-sparrow of a ruffian.

… 'I am now sir, muddied in Fortune's mood, and smell somewhat strong of her strong displeasure.'

I must say Helena is a terrifying female. Her virtue, her persistence, her pegging away after the odious Bertram (and disguised as a pilgrim – so typical!) and then telling the whole story to that *good* widow-woman! And that tame fish Diana. As to lying in Diana's bed and enjoying the embraces meant for Diana – well, I know nothing more sickening. It would take a respectable woman to do such a thing. The worst of it is I can so well imagine … for instance acting in precisely that way, and giving Diana a present afterwards. *What* a cup of tea the widow and D must have enjoyed while it was taking place, or did D at the last moment want to cry off the bargain? But to forgive such a woman! Yet Bertram would. There's an espèce de mothers-boyisme in him which makes him stupid enough for anything.

The Old King is a queer old card – he seems to have a mania for bestowing husbands. As if the one fiasco were not enough, Diana has no sooner explained herself than he begins:

> 'If thou be'st yet a fresh uncropped flower
> Choose thou thy husband, and I'll pay thy dower.'

I think Shakespeare must have seen the humour of that. It just – at the very last moment of the play, puts breath into the old fool.

'HAMLET'

Coleridge on Hamlet. 'He plays that subtle trick of pretending to act only when he is very near being what he acts.'

... So do we all begin by acting and the nearer we are to what we would be the more perfect our *disguise*. Finally there comes the moment when *we are no longer acting*; it may even catch us by surprise. We may look in amazement at our no longer borrowed plumage. The two have merged; that which we put on has joined that which was; acting has become action. The soul has accepted this livery for its own after a time of trying on and approving.

To act ... to see ourselves in the part – to make a larger gesture than would be ours in life – to declaim, to pronounce, to even exaggerate. To persuade ourselves? Or others? To put ourselves in heart? To do more than is necessary in order that we may accomplish ce qu'il faut.

And then Hamlet is lonely. The solitary person always acts.

But I could write a thousand pages about Hamlets.

Mad Scene. If one looks at it with a cold eye it really is poor. It depends entirely for its effect upon wispy Ophelia. The cardboard King and Queen are of course only lookers-on. They don't care a halfpenny. I think the Queen is privately rather surprised at a verse or two of her songs ... And who can believe that a solitary violet withered when that silly fussy old pomposity died? And who can believe that Ophelia really loved him, and wasn't thankful to think how peaceful breakfast would be without his preaching?

The Queen's speech after Ophelia's death is exasperating to one's sense of poetic truth. If no one saw it happen – if she wasn't found until she was drowned, how does the Queen know how it happened? Dear Shakespeare has been to the Royal Academy ... for his picture.

MIRANDA AND JULIET

To say that Juliet and Miranda might very well be one seems to me to show a lamentable want of perception. Innocent, early-morning-of-the-world Miranda, that fair island still half dreaming in a golden haze – lapped about with little joyful hurrying waves of love ... And small, frail Juliet, leaning upon the dark – a flower that is turned to the moon and closes, reluctant, at chill dawn. It is not even her spring. It is her time for dreaming: too soon for love. There is a Spring that comes before the real Spring and so there is a love – a false Love. It is incarnate in Juliet.

'ROMEO AND JULIET'

When the old nurse cackles of leaning against the dove-house wall it's just as though a beam of sunlight struck through the curtains and discovered her sitting there in the warmth with the tiny staggerer. One positively feels the warmth of the sunny wall ...

'TWELFTH NIGHT'

Malvolio's 'or ... play with some rich jewel.' There speaks the envious servant-heart that covets his master's possessions. I see him stroking the cloth with a sigh as he puts away his master's coat – holding up to the light or to his fingers the jewel before he snaps it into its ivory case. I see the servant copying the master's expressions as he looks in the master's mirror.

And that ... 'having risen from a day bed where I have left Olivia sleeping'. Oh, doesn't that reveal the thoughts of all those strange creatures who attend upon the lives of others!

'ANTONY AND CLEOPATRA'

Act I. Scene 1.
  'The triple pillars of the world ... '

'The wide arch of the ranged empire ... '
'To-night we'll wander through the streets and note The qualities
of people' (That is so *true* a pleasure of lovers.)

Act i. Scene 2.
    'A Roman thought hath struck him ... '
    'Ah, then we bring forth weeds
    'When our quick minds lie still ... '
Enobarbus constantly amazes me, *e.g.* his first speeches with
Antony about Cleopatra's celerity in dying.
    'Your old smock brings forth a new petticoat.'

Act i. Scene 3. Like Scene 2. (1) 'Saw you my lord?' (2) 'Where is he?'
'What says the *married* woman?' There's jealousy! And then her fury
that he's not more upset at Fulvia's death! 'Now I know how you'll
behave when I die!'
    These are beautiful lines of Antony's:
    'Our separation so abides and flies
    That thou, residing here, goes yet with me,
    And I, hence fleeing, here remain with thee.'

Act i. Scene 4.
    'Like to a vagabond flag upon the stream
    Goes to and back, lackeying the varying tide,
    To rot itself with motion.'
Marvellous words! I can apply them. There is a short story. And
then it seems that the weed gets caught up and then sinks; then it is
gone out to sea and lost. But comes a day, a like tide, a like occasion,
and it reappears more sickeningly rotten still! Shall he? Will he? Are
there any letters? No letters? The post? Does he miss me? No. Then
sweep it all out to sea. Clear the water for ever! Let me write this one
day.
    'Thy cheek so much as lanked not.' The economy of utterance.

Act i. Scene 5.
    'Now I feed myself with most delicious poison.'
    'An arm-gaunt steed?' Oh, yes; of course.

Act ii. Scene 1.
    '*Salt* Cleopatra ... '

Act II. Scene 2.

Enobarb: 'Every time serves for the matter that is born in it.'

Caesar: 'You praise yourself by laying defects of judgement to me, but you patch'd up your excuses.'

Enobarb: 'That truth should be silent; I had almost forgot.'

Act III. The short scene between Antony and the Soothsayer is very remarkable. It explains the tone of Caesar's remarks to Antony ... And Antony's concluding speech shows his uneasiness at the truth of it. He'll go to Egypt. He'll go where his weakness is praised for strength. There's a hankering after Egypt between the lines.

Scene 5. '*Tawny*-finned fishes ... their *shiny* jaws ... ' and the adjectives seem part of the nouns when Shakespeare uses them. They grace them so beautifully, attend and adorn so modestly, and yet with such skill. It so often happens with lesser writers that we are more conscious of the servants than we are of the masters, and quite forget that their office is to serve, to enlarge, to amplify the power of the master.

'Ram thou thy fruitful tidings in my ears

That long time have been barren.'

Good lines! And another example of the choice of the place of words. I suppose it was instinctive. But 'fruitful' seems to be just where it ought to be, to be resolved (musically speaking) by the word 'barren'. One reads 'fruitful' expecting 'barren' almost from the 'sound-sense'.

Cleo. 'Thou should'st come like a Fury crown'd with snakes

Not like a normal man.'

' "But yet" is as a jailor to bring forth

Some monstrous malefactor.'

There's matter indeed! Does not that give the pause that always follows those hateful words. 'But yet' – and one waits. And both look towards the slowly opening door. What is coming out? And sometimes there's a sigh of relief after. Well, it was nothing so very awful. The gaol-mouse, so to speak, comes mousing through and cleans his face with his paw.

'I am pale, Charmian.'

Reminds me of Mary Shelley. 'Byron had never seen any one so pale as I.' Something of John's too. I can't remember what. 'Was he as pale as she? He must have been for he felt the blood creeping back into his cheeks.' I don't know whether Bogey *wrote* creeping, or whether that's caricature. It makes me smile. It's *so* like him.

'Since I myself
Have given myself the cause.'
What does that mean exactly? That she sent Antony away? or let
Antony go?
    'In praising Antony I have dispraised Caesar ...
    I am paid for it now.'
A creature like Cleopatra always expects to be paid for things.

To Sydney and Violet Schiff, 3 December 1921

I have begun a certain amount of novel reviewing again[8] and oh –
the awful rubbish, the shameful stuff they send across! I read it; it
seems too bad to blame even – and then I read the reviews and find
Shaw Desmond is 'capable of a masterpiece, and well on the way of
writing one.' It is profoundly disquieting to be so out of touch with
one's times. I mean that very seriously. The only way to bear the
horrid truth is by writing oneself – going on ...

To Dorothy Brett, 5 December 1921

Wasn't that Van Gogh shown at the Goupil[9] ten years ago? Yellow
flowers, brimming with sun, in a pot? I wonder if it is the same. That
picture seemed to reveal something that I hadn't realized before I
saw it. It lived with me afterwards. It still does. That and another of a
sea-captain in a flat cap. They taught me something about writing,
which was queer, a kind of freedom – or rather, a shaking free.
When one has been working for a long stretch one begins to narrow
one's vision a bit, to fine things down too much. And it's only when
something else breaks through, a picture or something seen out of
doors, that one realizes it.

To Sydney Schiff, 28 December 1921

One word I must say about Joyce.[10] Having re-read the *Portrait* it
seems to me on the whole awfully *good*. We are going to buy *Ulysses*.
But Joyce is (if only Pound didn't think so too) immensely
important. Sometime ago I found something so repellent in his work
that it was difficult to read it – It shocks me to come upon words,
expressions and so on that I'd shrink from in life. But now it seems to
me the *new novel*, the seeking after Truth is so by far and away the
most important thing that one must conquer all minor aversions.
They are unworthy.

To Sydney Schiff, 15 January 1922

About Joyce, and my endeavour to be doubly fair to him because I have been perhaps unfair and captious. Oh, I can't get over a great great deal. I can't get over the feeling of wet linoleum and unemptied pails and far worse horrors in the house of his mind – He's so terribly *unfein*; that's what it amounts to. There is a tremendously strong impulse in me to beg him not to shock me! Well, it's not very rare. . . .

One can stand much, but that sort of shock which is the result of vulgarity and commonness, one is frightened of receiving. It's as though one's mind goes on quivering afterwards.

To Sydney Schiff, January 1922

Please do not think I am all for Joyce. I am *not*. In the past I was unfair to him and to atone for my stupidity I want to be fairer now than I really feel ... I agree that it is not all art. I would go further. Little, to me, is art at all. Its a kind of stage on the way to being Art. But the act of projection has not been made. Joyce remains entangled in it, in a bad sense, except at rare moments.

Journal, 17 January 1922

Tchehov made a mistake in thinking that if he had had more time he would have written more fully, described the rain, and the midwife and the doctor having tea. The truth is one can get only *so much* into a story; there is always a sacrifice. One has to leave out what one knows and longs to use. Why? I haven't any idea, but there it is. It's always a kind of race to get in as much as one can before it *disappears*.

But time is not really in it. Yet wait. I do not understand even now. I am pursued by time myself. The only occasion when I ever felt at leisure was while writing 'The Daughters of the Late Colonel'. And then at the end I was so terribly unhappy that I wrote as fast as possible for fear of dying before the story was sent.[11] I should like to prove this, to work at *real leisure*. Only thus can it be done.

To J. M. Murry, 7 February 1922

It's one of those books[12] which, once discovered, abides for ever. It's such a whole (even in part, as I have it). These two men live and one is carried with them. The slight absurdity and the sentimental bias of Eckermann I wouldn't have not there! Delightfully human – one smiles but one can't help smiling always tenderly. And then outside sounds come in – the bells of Weimar ringing in the evening – the whisper of the wheat as the friends walk together, the neighbours' little children calling like birds. But all this human interest (Ah! how it draws one) apart, there is Goethe talking, and he did say marvellous things. He was great enough to be simple enough to say what we all feel and don't say. And his attitude to Art was noble. It does me good to go to Church in the breasts of great men. Shakespeare is my Cathedral, but I'm glad to have discovered this other. In fact, isn't it a joy – there is hardly a greater one – to find a *new book*, a living book, and to know that it will remain with you while life lasts? . . .

I've read *Antony and Cleopatra* again last week, and upon my word it is appalling to find how much one misses each time in Shakespeare – how much is still new. Wonderful play! But, Bogey, you remember ' 'Tis one of those odd tricks which sorrow shoots out of the mind.' That is familiar enough, but it still leaves me gasping. There is something over and above the words – the meaning – all that I can see. It is that other language we have spoken of before. I feel that, as I am, I am not great enough to bear it. The image that for some reason comes into my mind is of an old woman in a cathedral, who bows down, folds herself up in her shawl, mournfully closes herself against the sudden stirring of the organ. You know when the organ begins and it seems to ruminate, to wander about the arches and the dark altars as though seeking some place where it may abide ...

To Dorothy Brett, 1 May 1922

[On *Ulysses*] . . . one needs to have a really vivid memory of the *Odyssey* and of English Literature to make it out at all. It's wheels within wheels within wheels. Joyce certainly had not one grain of a desire that one should read it for the sake of the coarseness, though I confess I find many a 'ripple of laughter' in it. But that's because (although I don't *approve* of what he's done) I do think Marion Bloom and Bloom are superbly seen at times. Marion is the complete complete female. There's no denying it. But one has to remember she's also Penelope, she is also the night and the day, she is also an image of the teeming earth, full of seed, rolling round and round.

To J. M. Murry, July 1922

Yes, Somerset Maugham lays it on too thick. It's too downright good a story – don't you think?[13] Too oily! And there's not enough rain in it. The rain keeps stopping. The whole story ought to have been soaked through and through – or steamed with the after the rain feeling. And it isn't and doesn't.

II   REVIEW MATERIAL FROM 1921

Review of To Let *by John Galsworthy*
('A Family Saga', Daily News, *5 November 1921; in full)*

A FAMILY SAGA

Mr Galsworthy's New Forsyte Novel

Philosophy of Faith in Love

After reading the last volume of the Forsyte saga we find ourselves wondering what would have been the reception of these books had they appeared as translations from the Russian, the Norwegian, or the Dutch. Not that the works of Mr Galsworthy suffer from neglect; his reputation as one of the foremost writers of our time is too securely established.

But perhaps there is a danger that, having made up our minds about him, we may, in our English way, cease to be curious. In these days when books are snatched at, glanced at, dipped into rather than read, we crave, as never before, the irritant of novelty. Well, our young writers are prolific enough to satisfy the most urgent appetite, and when their ever-increasing output has been devoured there are always the translations to tackle.

But here is a curious fact. In the case of the translations, though the bait may have been novelty, once we are caught nothing can exceed the patience, the absorbed attention, the sympathy with which we read a foreign author. Outlandish names, complicated relationships, have no terrors. And those longueurs which, were they genuine English longueurs, would exhaust our patience immediately, put into a foreign dress are all part of the fascination; we read, as though the age were returned when life was long and books were few.

THE FORSYTE BREED

Perhaps, at last, this passion for foreign travel will have its influence upon our behaviour at home. And instead of applying the familiar critical formula – 'sincere, distinguished, brilliant' – to the work of Mr Galsworthy, someone will discover how rich, how satisfying, how powerful, take it all in all, is this family piece hanging on our own walls.

Between *The Man of Property* and *To Let* there is contained the history of the rise and fall of the Forsyte family, told in such a way that we recognise it as the author's chosen subject – the subject of his heart, which all writers seek for but do not always find. In describing the Forsyte breed, typical English breed, with its tenacious jealous, passionately possessive grip on life, his gifts of irony and imaginative sympathy find their full expression.

Here, too, his dramatist's sense of character – so strong in Mr Galsworthy – is abundantly satisfied. But above all, the scope of his subject, the sense of the long time it takes for all these things to happen, enables him to convey his feeling for life. Life, relentless and mysterious, flows on for ever.

THE ONE UNBUYABLE THING

It is useless to deny it or to build up defences. It is almost comic to surround our impermanent selves with solidities, to hoard, to guard. We may linger long, we may relish our baked apple and worry about Consols to our hundredth year, but die we must. But how are we to bear this knowledge that all things have an end? How are we to accept this sense of the finality of things? His answer would seem to be by faith in nothing less than love. Love, the one thing worth having, was the one thing the Forsyte family could not buy. It flows from our bosoms and becomes part of that larger stream; it is beauty and the only immortality we shall ever know.

In *The Man of Property* the heart of the matter is the love of Soames Forsyte for Irene. He bought her; he made her his wife, his possession. And still he did not own her. Baffling and incredible situation for a Forsyte. Soames was, without doubt, the most typical of them all; the source of their power as a family seemed to be gathered up in him.

He was close, but he knew a good thing when he saw it. And he was the last man to be suspected of bringing shame upon the family's sound instinct for a speculation. But so it happened. In Irene he met his foe, and was beaten. *In Chancery* is the period between the battle and the fruits of that battle. In it Soames tries to recapture Irene, fails, and thinks to mend his broken life by marrying a healthy young Frenchwoman whom he expects to provide him with a son. Possessions – he must have possessions! His money and his pictures must feed the family passion.

THE SHOT BOLT

But Irene, who is married again to Jolyon, the artist of the Forsyte family, has a son. And the book ends with Soames at his river house hearing that life – for some extraordinary reason – has refused to be bought again. Annette's child is a girl.

The war is over. Soames is 65, with a grown-up daughter; Irene's boy is 19, with the opening of *To Let*. The little house in the Bayswater-road, cradle of the Forsytes, the house of the 'old people' of another century, another age, is deserted now, except for Timothy, in his 100th year. For him it has become a second cradle. There he lingers on, like a winter fly, with Smithers and Cook looking after him so beautifully, the last of the old Forsytes. No one goes to visit him now except Soames; the family has forgotten him. For it is strange. In these last years something has happened to that tenacious, solid, compact family. Soames feels its bolt is shot. Its day is over.

The possessive instinct is dying out. What has happened to the Forsyte ideal? It has come to nothing. Where are they all? Those warm, long-lived typical English men and women. They are dead or scattered. The family vault at Highgate has only room for Timothy. Soames, after a visit to the Bayswater-road house, after a prolonged tour of that perfect little Victorian museum, thinks of it, too, as a mausoleum. He lingers in the hall dreaming that some 'ghost of an old face might show over the banisters and an old voice say: "Why, it's dear Soames, and we were only saying that we hadn't seen him for a week!" '

THE FINAL TRAGEDY

Nothing – nothing! Just the scent of camphor, and dust-notes on a sunbeam through the fanlight over the door, ...

But there is a final struggle before the Forsyte family yields up its breath. While Timothy's soul is leaving its body Soames' final tragedy is enacted. His adored and once unwanted daughter, with her French name, 'Fleur', meets by chance Joss, the son of Irene, and the two promptly, at first sight, fall in love.

The idea is equally terrible to Soames and to Irene. But how are they to make those children of the present understand that it is the undying past that separates them for ever? It is done, and Joss, child of love, chooses his mother, and Fleur chooses another young man. But not before her father realises the bitter truth that he and his money are no use to her if they cannot buy love for her.

The book ends with Soames' last visit to Timothy in his new, neat, grey dwelling at Highgate. 'He sat there a long time, dreaming his career ... "To Let" – the Forsyte age and way of life ... "To Let" – that same [*sic*, for "sane"] and simple creed.' He is a tragic figure.

One does not know which to admire the more – the peculiar readiness and power with which Mr Galsworthy expresses the feelings which are aroused in us by the contemplation of what has been or the exquisite delicacy and freshness with which young love, first love, is depicted. Mr Galsworthy is affected by absent things as if they were present.

He can make us feel the past; we ache with it. *To Let* is haunted by ghosts – even the ghosts of portwine and camphor and stuffed humming-birds.

Notes

The following abbreviations are used throughout:

ATL   Alexander Turnbull Library, Wellington, New Zealand
Journal   *The Journal of Katherine Mansfield*, ed. J. M. Murry (1954)
LJMM   *Katherine Mansfield's Letters to J. Middleton Murry*, ed. J. Middleton
        Murry (1951)
NN   Katherine Mansfield, *Novels and Novelists* (New York, 1930)

Books published in London unless otherwise indicated.

INTRODUCTION

1. *LJMM*, p. 435 (8 Dec 1919).
2. Ibid., p. 283 (5 June 1918).
3. In conversation with the author, August 1983.
4. Michael Holroyd, *Lytton Strachey: A Critical Biography* (1968) II, 538.
5. *LJMM*, p. 4 (Summer 1913).
6. *The Letters and Journals of Katherine Mansfield*, ed. C. K. Stead (1977)
   p. 225 (June–July 1921).
7. *LJMM*, p. 614.
8. *Je ne parle pas français* (Hampstead: Heron Press, 1919).
9. Leonard Woolf, *Beginning Again: An Autobiography of the Years 1911–18*
   (1964) p. 204.
10. *NN*, p. 22.
11. ATL, MS Papers 119, Notebook 46.
12. The reference is to *Rhythm* (1911–13), which had for its slogan a phrase
    taken from Synge 'Before art can be human again it must learn to be
    brutal' (slightly misquoted from the Preface to Synge's *Poems and
    Translations*).
13. *LJMM*, pp. 612–13.
14. See *Journal*, p. 205, for a discussion of the artificial nature of 'the
    personal'.
15. *NN*, p. 314.
16. Ibid., pp. 112–13.
17. Ibid., p. 320.
18. Leonard Woolf, *Beginning Again*, p. 204.
19. A brief definition of terms: Symbolism capitalised is taken here to refer
    specifically to the Symbolist movement in French poetry towards the

end of the nineteenth century; symbolism (lower-case) is used more broadly to describe the twentieth-century post-Symbolist movement in European Literature.

20. The notes in this section of ATL Notebook 2 have not previously been traced to Symons's *Studies in Prose and Verse*. Critics who have made brief references to them, e.g. Vincent O'Sullivan in 'The Magnetic Chain: Notes and Approaches to KM', *Landfall*, 114 (1975) 95–131, have assumed that they are KM's own comments, whereas in fact almost every entry, with the exception of that quoted here, is taken virtually verbatim from Symons. ATL Notebook 8 also contains notes from Symons's *Plays, Acting and Music* (see Appendix 1).
21. ATL Notebook 2, fo. 58.
22. *LJMM*, pp. 392–3.
23. *NN*, p. 317.
24. *Journal*, p. 273.
25. Cf. Wordsworth's almost mystical sense of the beneficent powers of memory in *The Prelude*.
26. *NN*, p. 6.
27. Anthony Alpers, *The Life of Katherine Mansfield* (1980) p. 353.
28. *NN*, p. 236.
29. *NN*, p. 310.
30. *NN*, p. 178.
31. *NN*, pp. 44–5.
32. Letter of Katherine Mansfield to S. S. Koteliansky, British Library MS Add. 48970 (21 Aug 1919). The 'treasure' to which she refers is Russian literature in general, and, more specifically, the letters of Chekhov, which she and Koteliansky were currently translating.
33. The review (repr. in Ch. 2, pt II) has been accepted by KM scholars as being entirely by KM, but the internal evidence works strongly against this view.
34. Foreword to the 1938 edition of *Pilgrimage*, repr. in *Pilgrimage I* (Virago, 1979) p. 12.
35. Elaine Showalter, *A Literature of their Own* (1978) p. 246.
36. *NN*, p. 6.
37. Unpublished sketch, ATL Notebook 37, fos 8–14.
38. See, in this respect, Alpers, *The Life of Katherine Mansfield*, and C. A. Hankin, *The Confessional Stories of Katherine Mansfield* (1983).
39. Virginia Woolf's often cited hostile reaction to 'Bliss' should I think be referred to her own repressed feelings about lesbianism, and her unease over her perception of this theme in the story, in this respect more 'advanced' than anything she herself wrote.
40. See, for example, Sandra M. Gilbert and Susan Gubar (authors of *The Madwoman in the Attic*, 1979) in their article 'Sexual Linguistics: Gender, Language, Sexuality', *New Literary History*, 16.3 (Spring 1985) 515–43.

CHAPTER 1. THE WORLD OF TWO: KATHERINE MANSFIELD AND J. M. MURRY, 1911–19

1. *Confidence* (1880), James's fifth novel.
2. Presumably that edited by Sir Arthur Quiller-Couch (1900). *The Oxford Book of French Verse* (1907) was compiled by St John Lucas.
3. Léon Bloy (1846–1917), French novelist and mystical thinker.
4. *Signature* was a short-lived periodical (1915) in which, in D. H. Lawrence's words, he was to do the 'preaching', Murry to propound his 'ideas on freedom for the individual soul' and KM to write her 'little satirical sketches'. KM is referring here to the confessional style of Murry and Lawrence. This is the first of many occasions on which KM proved herself a devastating critic of Murry's work.
5. The *fauviste* painter J. D. Fergusson.
6. Cf. KM's *Athenaeum* review of Forster's *The Story of the Siren* (repr. in Ch. 2, pt II).
7. 'Geneva' and 'Hamilton' were stories never finished by KM, according to Murry, although sections of 'Geneva' exist in the ATL holdings. 'Hamilton' presumably refers to the town in New Zealand.
8. KM is quoting from 'The Love Song of J. Alfred Prufrock', l. 98. Cf. a letter to Virginia Woolf (?1917) in which she refers to Prufrock: 'Prufrock is after all a short story' – letter first published in *Adam International Review*, 370 (1972) p. 19. The latter remark sheds light on KM's conception of the short story as something which would have a lyric concentration and symbolist power akin to that of T. S. Eliot's poetry.
9. The Hon. Dorothy Brett, a painter who had studied at the Slade 1910–16.
10. Cf. D. H. Lawrence on Cézanne's apples in the essay 'Introduction to his Paintings'. KM, like D. H. Lawrence in his essay, is concerned with a Bergsonian 'ideal' moment of apprehension of that which lies outside the self. In such a moment some kind of fusion occurs between the self and the object contemplated, while, paradoxically, the self has at the same time a heightened sense both of its own identity and of the inalienable otherness of the object perceived.
11. By P. J. Toulet (1867–1920), French poet and novelist.
12. KM gives the line division wrongly here. The Shakespeare text reads:

> Will wing me to some withered bough, and there
> My mate, that's never to be found again
> Lament till I am lost.

> (*The Winter's Tale*, v. 3)

13. KM refers to *Eve's Ransom* (1895).
14. Cf. this passage with KM's later remarks on the 'undiscovered country' of prose (letter to Lady Ottoline Morrell (July 1916), see note 15).
15. Lady Ottoline Morrell, influential hostess and patroness of the arts, whose home at Garsington, near Oxford, became an important centre for artists and intellectuals during the First World War.
16. That is, for the Armistice in November 1918.

CHAPTER 2. 'WANTED, A NEW WORLD': THE *ATHENAEUM*, 1919–20

1. The *Athenaeum* was, as Anthony Alpers puts it, a 'languishing' weekly when Murry took over. The philanthropist Arnold Rowntree wanted to re-establish the paper to serve a new, post-war society: it was to be a 'Journal of Literature, Science, the Fine Arts, Music and Drama'.
2. Cf. Murry in a letter of 22 November 1919, in which he comments that KM, unlike Virginia Woolf, 'relates novels to life. Virginia can't abide that.'
3. 'Esther Waters Revisited', *Athenaeum*, 6 Aug 1920 (repr. in pt II of this chapter). The final image is from *As You Like It* (II. vii.39–40).
4. Those letters which bear directly on a review KM was writing are printed with the review in the second section of this chapter.
5. Chekhov's letters, tr. by the Russian emigré S. S. Koteliansky, aided by KM, were published in the *Athenaeum* from April to October 1919. They were originally to have been published as a book, but Constance Garnett beat Koteliansky and KM to press with her volume *The Letters of Anton Chekhov to his Family and Friends* in early 1920. See KM's letter of 21 August 1919 to Koteliansky for the influence on her of Chekhov's life and thought. She characterises his letters as 'this treasure – at the wharf only not unloaded' – a treasure which would revive the jaded English literary world (British Library MS 48970).
6. Sydney Waterlow, a cousin of KM's who had once proposed to Virginia Woolf.
7. An essay on Georges Duhamel (1884–1966), published in the *Athenaeum*.
8. Murry had become friendly with Walter de la Mare at this time, and KM refers to him affectionately in later letters.
9. KM's commentary is on Murry's book *The Evolution of an Intellectual*, a collection of essays and articles published in 1920.
10. Murry's note in *LJMM* runs, 'A review of Mr Festing Jones's *Life of Samuel Butler*, by Bernard Shaw, in *The Manchester Guardian*.' Murry would have sent the paper out to KM at Ospedaletti.
11. KM confuses the names 'Cheedle' and 'Meedle'. The reference is to *Our Mutual Friend*.
12. Cf. Ch. 1, note 10.
13. *Bliss, and Other Stories* (1920).
14. See also an *Athenaeum* review of KM's in which she characterises a new species of novel, the 'Garden City novel', with its 'brand-new exposed houses which seem to breathe white enamel and cork linoleum and the works of Freud or Jung' ('Two Modern Novels', *Athenaeum*, 9 Apr 1920).
15. *The Autobiography of Margot Asquith*, which both KM and Murry were reading. Cf. a letter of 4 November 1920, to Sydney and Violet Schiff, in which KM again compares Margot Asquith and Ottoline Morrell. This 'type' of the *artiste manqué* was one which fascinated KM. Her most ruthless analysis of such a character appears through the portrayal of Bertha Young in 'Bliss'.

16. Sydney and Violet Schiff, two wealthy patrons of the arts, with whom KM became friendly during her stay in Menton in the early months of 1920 (they later had a villa at Roquebrune, near Menton). Sydney Schiff had published a novel, under the name of Stephen Hudson, which KM had earlier reviewed for the *Athenaeum*, not knowing the true identity of the author. As Stephen Hudson, Schiff later translated into English the final volume of *À la recherche du temps perdu*. This letter is previously unpublished (BL MS 52919).

17. Cf. Murry in 'The Daughter of Necessity', an essay in *The Evolution of an Intellectual* (1920): 'The true creation of art begins thus with the complete assertion of surrender' (p. 57).

18. For KM's use of Coleridge's phrase 'anatomy of description instead of creative power' see also the 1920 journal notes on Coleridge. Cf. also KM's early notebook entries (see Appendix 1) on the 'partisans of analysis' as opposed to those who use the true artist's 'objective' method, describing the state of the soul 'through the slightest gesture'. Her preference for the symbolist method of conveying abstract states of mind or feeling through concrete symbols remained constant.

19. A story written at Menton, November 1920, which Murry had declined for the *Athenaeum*, finding it 'not wholly successful'. KM's masterly defence of the story again spells out her symbolist aim to reveal the abstract through the concrete 'the slightest gesture' – 'these are the rapid confessions one receives sometimes from a glove or a cigarette or a hat'.

20. For the reference here, see Introduction, note 12.

21. KM is discussing the essays in Murry's collection *Aspects of Literature* (1920).

22. Alpers, *The Life of Katherine Mansfield*, p. 294.

23. *The Letters of John Middleton Murry to Katherine Mansfield*, ed. C. A. Hankin, p. 210.

24. The fourth novel in the *Pilgrimage* series.

25. The relationship, if any, between KM's 1917 descriptions of the garden at Garsington and Virginia Woolf's prose poem *Kew Gardens* remains obscure. In August 1917 KM wrote about the garden to both Ottoline Morrell and Virginia Woolf in terms which seem to anticipate Woolf's story – she described, for example, 'several *pairs* of people – their conversation their slow pacing – their glances as they pass one another – the pauses as the flowers "come in" as it were' (letter to Ottoline Morrell, 15 Aug 1917). KM first read *Kew Gardens* in the same month, and later in August wrote to Woolf, 'Yes, your Flower Bed is *very* good. Theres a still, quivering, changing light over it all and a sense of those couples dissolving in the bright air which fascinates me – '.

26. *The Arrow of Gold* was in fact a late work: KM's response to the novel seems in retrospect to accord with the current view that Conrad's later work shows a marked decline in his powers.

27. Alpers, *The Life of Katherine Mansfield*, p. 445.

28. The fifth novel in the *Pilgrimage* series.

29. The penultimate novel completed by Conrad.

30. As Anthony Alpers points out (Alpers, *The Life of Katherine Mansfield*,

p. 294) in this serious and searching review of Forster, KM makes amends for the gibe about Leonard Bast's umbrella (see 1917 journal entry on Forster, repr. in Ch. 1, pt II; KM had earlier tried out the remark in the *New Age*).

31. KM seriously misjudges Gertrude Stein: see Introduction for a discussion of her relationship to 'feminine prose'.

32. This note was in KM's copy of *Aaron's Rod*. Murry presumably linked it with his collection of *Athenaeum* material thinking it would not otherwise be published. See the note in the text for Murry's anxiety to establish himself and KM as admirers of Lawrence.

33. The *Dial* was an American periodical edited at this time by Scofield Thayer and James Sibley Watson, Jr. Lawrence was a regular contributor between 1920 and 1925.

34. This letter is also previously unpublished except in *Adam International Review*, 300 (1965) p. 112.

35. Couperus (1863–1923) is a novelist now valued less for the exotic elements of his art (e.g. in plot and setting) than for his skill in observing minutiae and in painting mood. It is this second aspect of his work which seems to have attracted KM.

36. In this sympathetic and perceptive view of Hamsun's best-known novel, KM seems ahead of her time. Hamsun's reputation is only now recovering from the set-back it received because of his pro-Nazi attitude in the Second World War.

37. May Sinclair (1863–1946) was a novelist, essayist and great admirer of the work of Dorothy Richardson. She was the first writer to use the term 'stream of consciousness' (borrowed from William James) to denote a literary method – this in an enthusiastic article on Richardson. In that her technique is rather similar to that of Richardson, it is perhaps not surprising that she came under attack from KM. Murry reported in 1920 that he had been told May Sinclair 'had been terribly upset by KM's review of her novel, because she thought that KM [was] the only person who really knows how to do it' (*The Letters of John Middleton Murry to Katherine Mansfield*, ed. Hankin, p. 280).

38. Sheila Kaye-Smith, Rose Macaulay, Rhoda Broughton and Catherine Carswell are among the writers whose works are currently being reprinted in the Virago Modern Classics series.

39. See note 38.

40. Catherine Carswell (1870–1946), novelist and biographer, was one of D. H. Lawrence's most loyal friends, and was known to KM. See John Carswell, *Lives and Letters* (1978). In 1932 she published a biography of Lawrence, *The Savage Pilgrimage*, which was intended to be a response to Murry's *Son of Woman*, and which contained a savage attack on Murry and his claims to be able to speak 'for' Lawrence.

41. See note 38.

42. Note KM's singling out of the image of the party here, used in a sense rather different from that of Virginia Woolf, for whom the party was a positive image, figuring human communion. For KM too the party was an image of brightness and pleasure, but it has darker undertones and shadows. What is bright is also transient: KM became acutely aware of

this through her own illness and through the wider horror of the war. See the story 'The Garden Party', which is, as its title suggests, in a sense a 'war' story: one of its buried themes is the death in the war of KM's brother.

43. See note 42.

44. This is virtually the only 'manifesto' KM produced for the kind of fiction she herself wrote, and it is noticeable that she can only define it in negative terms or, as she puts it, 'in the form of a riddle'. She states categorically that 'it' is 'not a short story': see my *Short Stories and Short Fictions, 1880–1980* (1985) for the argument that KM was one of the most important modernist writers to develop the form of 'short fiction' as opposed to the plot-based 'short story'. The specific texts named by KM as 'models' are of course by Chekhov.

45. Ironically, Elizabeth Robins, a prominent feminist writer, had been admired by KM in her youth: one of her earliest journal entries reads 'I have just finished reading a book by Elizabeth Robins, *Come and Find Me*. Really, a clever, splendid book; it creates in me such a sense of power. I feel that I do now realise, dimly, what women in the future will be capable of' (*Journal*, p. 36).

46. KM makes private reference here to her New Zealand past. The 'Molesworth family' lived at Karori, where KM spent the most important part of her childhood. 'Old Anderson' is a variant on an outsider-figure also remembered from childhood: see further the story 'Ole Underwood', first published in *Rhythm*.

47. Jane Mander's *The Story of a New Zealand River* is generally thought to be a milestone in the development of the New Zealand novel. KM's relative harshness may be due to the fact that she herself was after a rather different kind of 'New Zealand' literature, which would overcome or pass beyond the felt gap between the old culture and the new – 'Oh, I want for one moment to make our undiscovered country *leap into the eyes of* the Old World' she wrote in 1916 (*Journal*, p. 94, emphasis added).

48. See letter to J. M. Murry of 25 September 1920, repr. in pt ɪ of this chapter.

49. This letter to the Schiffs is also previously unpublished (BL MS 52919).

50. 'The Stranger'.

CHAPTER 3. WORK IN PROGRESS: NOTES ON WRITING, 1921–2

1. Arthur (Richard) Murry was Middleton Murry's younger brother, at this time studying at the General School of Art and Design.

2. KM uses the word 'slave' in the Chekhovian sense, meaning that ignoble part of oneself which one deliberately drives out (it should be noted that Chekhov also used the word in a spirit of some irony, as he was himself the grandson of a serf).

3. Both stories written for the *Sphere*. Clement Shorter commissioned six

stories in July 1921: these were written 'against time' and not one of them was considered by KM to be among her best work.

4. Cf. the letter to Virginia Woolf of May 1919, repr. in Ch. 1, pt I.

5. William Gerhardi (later Gerhardie) was a novelist and critic. KM responded to his letters at this time, when he was a young and aspiring writer, with a nicely judged blend of kindness and criticism. *Futility* was, Gerhardie says, 'overhauled' along the lines KM suggested before it was first published (with KM's help) in 1922. It has been reissued as a Penguin Modern Classic.

6. Subsequently translated as *The Philosophy of 'As If'*, by C. K. Ogden. In her translation of Vaihinger and expansion of his ideas, KM develops a theme which had been implicit in some of her earlier comments about art. Just as Vaihinger sees a sharp distinction between thought and existence, thought having its autonomous laws and nature distinct from those of existence, so KM suggests there is an equally firm distinction between the world of art and 'reality' (which she takes to indicate both Vaihinger's 'thought' and 'existence'). Art may be a means to life, and may minister to life, but this does not mean that the artist must confuse the two spheres or attempt to *impose* his vision on life. The aim of the artist may further be summed up as an attempt to express truth rather than reality in the sense of 'what we accept as reality'.

7. Both KM and Murry kept – irregularly – their 'Shakespeare notebooks' (see *LJMM*, p. 653).

8. For the *Daily News*, and perhaps also for the *Nation*.

9. KM refers to the First Post-Impressionist Exhibition, organised by Roger Fry – but she has mistaken her gallery. The exhibition was mounted at the Grafton Galleries.

10. Cf. KM's conflicting statements on Joyce with Virginia Woolf's rather similar reactions, recorded in her letters and diary. Both writers recognised immediately the importance of Joyce, but seem to have felt somewhat threatened by the appearance of *Ulysses*, that battleship on the ocean of literature. After a meeting with KM and Murry in February 1922, Joyce remarked, according to Violet Schiff, that KM 'seemed to understand his book better than her husband' (who had just written an article on it).

11. See D. Kleine, 'Mansfield and the Orphans of Time', *Modern Fiction Studies*, 24.3 (1978–9), for a sensitive discussion of the themes of time and mortality in 'The Daughters of the Late Colonel'.

12. The edition KM would have been most likely to use is *Eckermann: Gespräche mit Goethe, Selections*, ed. R. F. Patterson (1907).

13. 'Rain' (Murry's note, *LJMM*, p. 657).

Appendix 1: Material from Katherine Mansfield's Early Notebooks*

The material here has been transcribed from holograph notebooks in the possession of the Alexander Turnbull Library, Wellington, New Zealand. I have included all that which seems relevant to the evolution of the author's aesthetic and critical point of view. While portions of the early notebooks have been published by J. Middleton Murry (in the 1954 *Journal*) the material here transcribed has not previously been published. Much of it consists of notes taken by KM from the works of other writers. It may be assumed that she copied these notes verbatim unless stated otherwise.

I FROM NOTEBOOK 1, ATL MANSFIELD MSS

Notebook 1 is the 'Juliet' notebook, containing this early novel and other story fragments, e.g. 'The Tale of the Three', 'Summer Idylle 1906'. It was begun in 1906, and there seem to be no entries later than mid 1908, i.e. about the time of KM's departure from New Zealand.

Fo. 129v

Poems of the Apostle of Youth[1] –

1. Late in the night – I lie on my bed, & press my face into the pillow. Oh, how strong I feel – like a giant even – and far too happy to sleep –

---

* In reproducing material from Katherine Mansfield's early notebooks I have tried to be as faithful as possible to the original notes, preserving their freshness and spontaneity, especially in matters of layout. – [ed.]
[1] These 'poems' are interesting precisely because they are not poems but prose-poems, exercises in prose phrasing. Cf. the later 'Vignettes' and 'Silhouettes'.

2. Now is the winter gone – and the first crocus – lights its warm lamp upon the barren earth –
3. Kneeling by the stream – I watch a brown leaf float float ~~down~~[2] the shining water – oh little brown leaf – whither – whither?
4. Often at midnight I open my window – and there wanders in my room many a ghostly visitant – Welcome – I love to feel your airy kisses upon my hot mouth.
5. A briar rose is swinging in the blue day. But a wind comes and the blossom is shattered. Strange – that it should be far more beautiful as it trails in the dust.

II FROM NOTEBOOK 2, ATL MANSFIELD MSS

Notebook 2 was begun about 14 November 1907 and taken to London in June 1908. The last dated entry is April 1909.

Fos 49v–50r[3]

CHARLES DICKENS 1812–

egalitarian = the egalitarian French Rev. idea – tends to produce great men.
Our meals, our manners and our daily lives are random symbols of the soul – p. 16
By simply going on being absurd a thing can become Godlike!
there is but one step from the ridiculous to the sublime!   p. 21
Dream for one mad moment that the grass is green   28
It is from the backs of the elderly gentlemen that the wings of the butterfly should burst.   p. 35
moor effoc[4]
his soul was a shot silk of black and crimson not a mingled colour of grey and purple
[Fo.50r] Youth is almost everything else – but original – pragmatical =
de minimis non curat lex =
Manners those grand rhythms of the social harmony   p127.

[2] KM's deletion.
[3] Notes from G. K. Chesterton, *Charles Dickens* (1906).
[4] Dickens mentioned a coffee shop which he frequented in his youth – this represents the inscription on the back, read backwards on the wrong side. Chesterton cites this as an example of Dickens's ability to isolate the significant detail, here 'endowed with demoniac life'.

Fo.58[5]
(inverted)

The partisans of analysis describe minutely the state of the soul; the secret motive of every action as being of far greater importance than the action itself. The partisans of objectivity – give us the result of this evolution sans describing the secret processes. They evoke the state of the soul through the slightest gesture – i.e. realise flesh covered bones – which is the artists method for me – In as much as art seems to me *pure vision* – I am indeed a partisan of objectivity – Yet I cannot take the simile of the soul and the body for there is [*fo.58v*; inverted] no body framework – supposing the bones were not bones but liquid Light – which suffuses itself – fluctuates – Well and Good – but the two are permanent and changeless ∴ the [?]failure

Fo.66v–67v[6]

1799–1850

Balzac 'La passion est toute l'humanité'
In him, as in all great artists there is something more than nature, a divine excess. *an overplus* – His supreme passion is the passion of *Will*. His creations are full of fire, each man and each woman – called by name responds as does King Lear or Hamlet. He is concerned with the senses through the intellect – his style is by no means perfect – the stylist sees life through coloured glass – Balzac deals in the elemental passions & desires – and *money* is with him a symbol – not an entity – Here is the thesis of the Human Comedy:–

First effects
Second causes
Third Principles
Essai sur les forces humaines –
filled with the joy of creation.

---

[5] Notes on Arthur Symons, *Studies in Prose and Verse* (1904). This is the only passage in KM's notes from Symons that is not directly quoted, though the argument develops out of some remarks of Symons on the 'novel of analysis' as against the 'objective study' (pp. 6–7).
[6] Notes from Symons, *Studies in Prose and Verse*. The Balzac notes are from pp. 5–25.

[*Fo.67r*] he lived most vividly – he loved 2 women
the second whom he married Madame de Hanska was the Beatrice
to his Dante.
Balzac is colossal.

Prosper Mérimée – attendrissement une fois par an –
'In history I care only for anecdote'
There is always with him this union of *curiosity* with *indifference* –
student curiosity & the indifference of the man of the world.

De Quincey – a tangled attempt to communicate the incommunicable
– his narrative like a worm – turning back upon itself as it moves – his
prose is shouted from the platform –

Nathaniel Hawthorne he is with Tolstoi the only novelist of the soul –
he is concerned with what is abnormal – 'was plucked up out of a
mystery – and had its roots still clinging to her'.[7]
His people are dream creatures faintly conscious that they dream
[*fo.67v*] they too often substitute fancy for imagination
'His feeling for flowers was very exquisite – & seems not so much a
taste as an emotion'
Writes with his nerves – [?] which I agree?

Walter Pater an exquisite fineness
'[Il a] rêvé le miracle d'une prose poétique musicale sans rhythme et
sans rime'
Philosophy is a sympathetic appreciation of a kind of music in the
very nature of things (*Plato & Platonism*)

RLS[8] a literary vagrant –
True style is *not* the dress but the *flesh* of the thought – 'He awakens
the eternal spirit of romance, even in the bosoms of the
conventional'

Flaubert – nous ne suivons plus la même route, nous ne navignons
plus dans la même vaisselle,[9] Non,! je ne cherche pas le port – mais
la haute mer.

[7] Symons quotes Hawthorne as saying this of one of his women
characters.
[8] Robert Louis Stevenson.
[9] 'la même vaisselle': *sic*, for 'le même vaisseau'.

Fos 81–79[10]

[*Fo.81r*] 'Whatever actually occurs is spoiled for art.'
Wilde – in his essay on Wainewright says 'it is only the Philistine who seeks to measure a personality by the vulgar test of production. Life itself is an Art.'
'A truth in art is that whose contradictory is also true.'
Wilde – as Symons so aptly says was the 'supreme artist in intellectual attitudes'

To the Italian Love 'comes from a root in Boccaccio – through the stem of Petrarch – to the flower of Dante. And so he becomes the idealist of material things, instead of the materialist of spiritual things – <Like Wilde – and like Beardsley –> the spirit is known only through the body – the body is but clay in the shaping or destroying hands of the spirit.' <'Soul and senses – senses and soul' – here is the inmost spirit of Henry Wooton – here is the quintessence [*fo.80v*] of Wilde's Life – of Dowson – and (Good God! What a creature) of Arthur Symons two most vitally interesting books of Poems – to Pater – this did not so exactly apply – yet there is a very real sensuousness in his earliest Portraits – a certain voluptuous pleasure in garden scents.>[11]
'Well, nature is immoral – Birth is a grossly sexual thing …[12]
Death is a grossly physical thing'
The Renaissance cultivated personality as we cultivate orchids – striving after a heightening of natural beauty which is art not nature – a perversity which may be poisonous … <'KM says the *intensity* of an action is its truth' –>
'not everyone can become the artist of his own life – or have the courage to go his own way.'
D'annunzio [*sic*] cannot imagine beauty without a pattern –
Is a thing the expression of an individuality?[13]

---

[10] Folios used in reverse order. Notes from Symons, *Studies in Prose and Verse*. Angle brackets indicate KM's own interpolations and comments.
    [11] Aside from KM's interpolations, the preceding passage quotes from Symons's essay on d'Annunzio. She returns to this in the next quotation.
    [12] This phrase is wrongly attributed to Katherine Mansfield herself in V. O'Sullivan, 'The Magnetic Chain: Notes and Approaches to KM', *Landfall*, 114 (1975) pp. 95–131. This leads I think to a mistaken emphasis on her early psychosexual problems.
    [13] Symons is discussing criteria for the inclusion of detail in art.

[*Fo.80r*] Mallarmé
'La chair est triste, hélas! et j'ai lu tous les livres'
For the principles of Art are eternal – the principles of Morality ebb
and flow even with the *climate*. Whatever I find in humanity is part
of the eternal substance which nature weaves for Art to combine
into a beautiful pattern –

The Moods of Men – Whatever has existed has achieved the right to
artistic existence. <But experience is not everything much depends
on the experimentalist>[14]

Formal art is so apt to be the enemy of artists – Symons.
Mérimée has les idées très arrêtées
the artist becomes an artist by the intensification of Memory-
extraneous –
It is the clear sighted sensitiveness of a man who watches human
things closely, bringing them home to himself with the deliberate
essaying art of an [*fo.79v*] actor who has to represent a particular
passion in movement.

<Now I do really want to write. There is silence – peace save for the
dull murmur of the sea – the sea almost as Little Paul[15] likes it – There
is the island – the sea ripples up against the beach so passive – so
beautiful. Ah! quelle joie.>

Zola defines Art as nature seen through a temperament (drives in a
victoria to see the peasants)[16]

Maupassant –
his abundant vitality.
Great artists are those who can make men see their particular
illusion <(That is true with limitations). The partisans of analysis
describe minutely the state of the soul – the secret motives of every
action – as being of infinitely greater importance than the action
itself[17]

[14] Much of the preceding is taken from Symons's Preface (repr. in *Studies
in Prose and Verse*) to his book of poems *London Nights*.
[15] In *Dombey and Son*.
[16] Symons quotes this story to illustrate Zola's lack of real knowledge of
his subjects.
[17] Against this passage KM has written 'Balzac'.

[*Fo.79r*] *The partisans of objectivity* give us the result of the evolution without describing the secret processes – he makes his characters so demean themselves that their slightest gesture shall be the expression of their souls. ∴ there is whole colour. It is a portrait – but the flesh covers the bones – >

He[18] was trained under the severe eye of Flaubert
'the light soul of the champagne flew off in tiny bubbles'

Philosophy of George Meredith
Memoirs of the 15th century Paston[19]

III   FROM NOTEBOOK 8, ATL MANSFIELD MSS

Notebook 8 was begun in October 1908 after Katherine Mansfield's return to London, and the last dated entry is for 29 February 1912.

The first two fragments are interesting for the way they show KM, as early as 1908, using the sea image for herself as an artist and dwelling on the importance of memory. The sea image continues through her journals and is finally connected explicitly with memory in a letter to Murry on Fitzherbert Terrace, Wellington.[20]

Fo.4r

he thrills in the memory.: I am like a harp if one listens eye shut & deeply enough one hears that strange ringing which with years of sweeping waves grows fainter and more forlorn – and yet is there – I am like a shell murmuring of the restless tides – and the troubled passion of the deep sea.

Fo.7r[21]

The feeling of dark strength in picture ... as I would hold a lost love with passion & terror & and the melancholy of memory. Memory is an oasis in the mirage of the present.

[18] Maupassant.
[19] These clearly intended as books for reading.
[20] *LJMM*, p. 511.
[21] After 'memories of New Zealand'.

Fo.8v[22]

> And Mr Wells has got a play
> upon the English stage
> about Arnold Bennett comes from where
> They make the pretty mugs
> I was a draper in my time
> And now I'm all the rage
> My name is Mr H. G. Wells
> And Kipps is on the stage
>
> I'm Arnold Bennett L[S?]D

Fo.25v[23]

Oh Kathie je veux écrire quelque chose d'immense – mais c'est bien difficile – even so Death is preferable to barrenness.
Such is your idea of a good book.
Born in New Zealand in W'gton the country the storm – the esplanade – the bedroom – then old Mrs [illegible name, ?Masparaty] – the M[other] dies at birth so the child is brought up by the grandmother. The Father a shrewd man of business – no other children. The journey to the country and cousins Aunt Miriam – Private school life – and journey to England with the Father. Left there at college – meeting with [illegible]

Fo.24r[24]

It is only interesting in parts. Make it psychological & place the school stay at Harley Street.

Fo.35v[25]

Why can I not write a happy story very much in the style of the Love Episode – in the house of Milly Green – Let me think out a really fine

---

[22] The beginnings of a parody of the realists Bennett and Wells, perhaps intended for the *New Age*. The date 29 February 1912 and a reference to 'Biggy B' (i.e. Beatrice Hastings, co-editor of the *New Age*, occur on fo. 9r.

[23] Story outlines.

[24] Commenting on preceding story outline.

[25] In the middle of the 'Miriam' story, which deals with the issue of women's role, and belongs to 1908.

plot and then slog at it – and get it ended today – it would do me worlds of good & Lesley would be so delighted – come, surely that is not hard. Something a little sordid for why I cannot tell I'm rather good at that style of thing – Have a child in it – a wunderkind – have a coffee stall in it – 'sleepy eyes and a poisonous voice'.

Fos48v, 47v, 46v, 45v[26]

ARTHUR SYMONS

I wish to make a little selection for future reference ...
He drew the melody from the violin as one draws the perfume from a flower, with a kind of slumbrous ecstasy misunderstood notation reading it like a cryptogrammatist he diverts one in upon a house of dreams full of intimate & ghostly voices[27]

In the music of Wagner there is that breadth and universality by which emotion ceases to be personal and becomes elemental. He stood, as the music seemed to foam about him, as a rock against which the foam beats
[*Fo.47v*] The music of Wagner has human blood in it. What Wagner tried to do is to unite mysticism and the senses, to render mysticism through the senses – that is what Rossetti tried to do in painting – that insatiable crying out of a carnal voice
And that feeling of Chopin – the dew as well as the rain has a sound for him –

Parsifal – Light
Tristan – Sea
Ring – Fire

it is a sea change – the Life of the foam in the life of the depths.
caress you like the fur of a cat –
we have blind vengeance, aged
Maeterlinck[28]

---

[26] Folios used in reverse order. Notes from Arthur Symons, *Plays, Acting and Music* (1903, rev. edn 1909), a collection of essays.
[27] On Dolmetsch.
[28] KM has jotted the name down in the midst of notes from Symons on Maeterlinck.

[*fo.46v*] and helpless wisdom; we have the conflict of passions fighting in the dark, destroying what they desire most in the world.

Strauss   Don Juan – passion, & loneliness. All the notes of the music evaporated like bubbles.

Oscar was a philosopher in masquerade.

KM Memory is a garden and the flowers in it are immortal –
<immortelles – everlasting flowers – dry as dust & leafless. It seems that every S. evening at nine o'clock I must go and meet you my beloved.>[29]
The sea cry is the doctrine of more abundant life, of unlimited freedom, of an unknown ecstasy – you do not necessarily get to your [*fo.45v*] destination by taking the right turning at the beginning of the journey –

Even the American daughter might take her Mother to see it[30] – without corrupting the innocence of old age –

Mozart music sans le désir content with beauty. It has the fine lines of a Durer picture – or of Botticelli – compared with the Titian splendour of Wagner. There is the romantic suggestion of magic in this beauty.

---

[29] KM's interpolation.
[30] A play by Alfred Capus, *Les Deux Ecoles*.

Appendix 2: 'Virginia's Journal'

'Virginia's Journal' (*Rhythm*, January 1913) is a clever parody in the style of the epistolary novel, attacking aspects of London literary life. It was written at the time of a running feud between Murry's magazine *Rhythm* and A. R. Orage's *New Age*. The *New Age* had been the first paper to publish KM's work, and her defection to *Rhythm* was bitterly resented. Beatrice Hastings, Orage's co-editor and an erstwhile friend of KM, launched a series of vicious, and anonymous, attacks on *Rhythm* in 1912. 'Virginia's Journal', also unsigned, is a clear hit back at the *New Age* and its circle of contributors. References to Orage and his friends abound: first in the prominent mention of the 'Tea House in the City' – the favourite haunt of the *New Age* contributors was the ABC teashop in Chancery Lane. The idea of the writer who has published 'Papers in Praise of a Philosopher, whom he declared yesterday he has since grown out of' could relate to any number of the younger *New Age* contributors, for example T. E. Hulme; while the references to 'Classical Learning' of a rather pointless kind seem to be a direct hit at Orage and J. M. Kennedy, both of whom tended to rely on classical allusions to pad out their writing and conversation.

'Virginia's Journal', not previously identified as being by KM, shows her quick spirit and impatience of stereotypes: it reads as though it is entirely her work, with no 'Murry influence'. It is interesting to note that criticism of Bennett ('Rennet') was common, or commonplace, by 1913, long before the publication of Woolf's 'Mr Bennett and Mrs Brown' (1924). The irony of this particular attack on Bennett is compounded by the fact that Bennett was himself a respected contributor to the *New Age* (under the pseudonym Jacob Tonson).

VIRGINIA'S JOURNAL

I cannot but wish, my dear Isabel, that you had left your dear Mama and journey'd with me to this Wondrous City. For indeed it is more full of marvels daily, and I am fearful to think that I must so soon return to my home and have nothing of it remaining but *Fragrant Memories*, united to a pang in the heart that is no longer wholly mine! But of this I shall speak later ... Suffice it to say that I have not one string alone to my bow, and I am daily in such *distinguished* companies that I am compell'd to wear my Indian Muslins from Morning to Night. Aunt says she has never seen a Shade more suited to my Eyes and Hair! But I am not mindful to write of Frivolity, my dear Isabel. – Indeed, were I to remain longer in my present surroundings, I think I should forsake all thought of Men and Matrimony and comb the curls out of my hair (were that not impossible) and bid my maid make me a grey woollen gown with a wide pocket such as we *detest*, and become an Intellectual Female! I am certain that had Papa not laugh'd so hearty (which was wrong in him) at my childish attempts to con the Classics; I should have succumb'd to their Fascinations. It is *lamentable* to what Confusion one can be put for one's ignorance of Great Men! And that is not all. I now see clearly the shocking harm Mama has done in locking the door of the library against me when I would have read the books by the Famous Authors of our own times. (Burn this after you have read it.) It would seem that there has never been so great and so distinguish'd a company of Authors as is at this time in London, and a Knowledge of their Works is – as Aunt's Journal has it – as important to the modern reader as Life or Death!

You will laugh at my Seriousness, my dear Isabel, but *pray, pray* do not do so.

Yesterday I went with Uncle to a Tea House in the City to meet a Mr Crawley from the country (except twice in the week when he resides in London) and a Mr Bloom who is a very stout, pale gentleman in tight trousers. Mr Crawley has publish'd two Papers in Praise of a Philosopher, whom he declared yesterday he has since grown out of – and is embarked upon a Book which all declare will create a Mighty Stir on account of the strange Lack of all Female Characters. Not a Frill or a Flutter of a Petticoat, my dear Isabel! He confess'd yesterday that he has since – I don't know when – grown out of them, also! Indeed he is what a sea-faring Friend of Uncle's is pleased to call a *Rum Shark*! Mr Bloom – who displeased me mightily by tickling my hand unobserved when Uncle presented him (which I cannot account for now except that he is the victim of a nervous complaint, he being so serious afterwards), has spent the greater part of his Life in Continental Travelling. He told a Story yesterday which fill'd me with Astonishment to the effect that when he was travelling in Paraguay he was mistook for the King of Spain. 'But, Sir,' said Uncle, 'I fail to see, I fail entirely to see … ' Whereupon Mr Bloom fell a laughing and as sudden became grave. 'They did not see me,' said he, 'but only the Lady with whom I was travelling!' This, winking at Mr Crawley, who smiled in an Abashed Manner and knocked out his Tobacco Pipe. I think that Uncle was offended that Mr Bloom should speak thus in my Hearing for he *turn'd the Conversation*, as they say in London – and it is most apt – to Modern Literature. 'Pray Sir,' he said to Mr Crawley, 'and what is your opinion of Mr Rennet?' Mr Crawley replied as quick as little Miss reciting Catechism. 'I think Mr Rennet hath a certain facility of technique, which facility hath no virtue since it is entirely mechanical, and floweth with the ease of water from a Bath-Cock rather than a stream down a mountain. Mr Rennet hath no true understanding of the Essentials. If he is taking you to the Death-Bed of his Hero he must needs make you stumble over a Brown Dog on the Door Mat and swear that this tripping is more than objective, or realistic, or naturalistic. And Mr Rennet's ignorance of the Poetics, Sir, of Aristotle and the Universal Consciousness is such that ... in short ... ' – here he faltered and said no more, but calling a serving maid order'd a Portion of Luncheon Cake.

My dear Isabel, you can imagine how edified I felt to be listening to such *Pearls of Wisdom!* But Uncle seemed out of Humour still on account of that Silly Jest of Mr Bloom's, for he retorted, 'I fail to see, Sir, how you can dismiss Mr Rennet so lightly, seeing that he hath made a fortune out of his writings and is paid, I have heard, at the Rate of Several Shillings a Word for all that he makes public, and even his private Correspondents – both here and in the United States of America – dispatch him Half-a-Crown or a Dollar Bill for every answer he may send, it being appropriated by him for a Statue of himself which is being erected out of China in a Pottery Works to the North. I cannot but count him as one of our Ablest Men.'

'Speaking of pottery,' quoth Mr Bloom, 'reminds me of a gem – a gem of a Poem which I have just found and translated from the Greek. I am so delighted with it that I have gone about all day repeating it to my Friends and to myself and to any one who perceiveth a Cultural Atmosphere. Alas! How few! And all Foreigners!' 'Pray let us hear it without delay', cried Mr Crawley. And Mr Bloom repeated – 'Stop his Spouting; if not, break his China!' He and Mr Crawley were so vastly amused at this Comick Poem that I endeavoured to smile, my dear Isabel, but for the Life of me I could not see the *beauty* of this Jewel! 'Ah!' said Mr Crawley, blowing his nose upon a spotted Handkerchief, 'What is the use of saying Anything when Everything hath been said to such

Perfection!' *Habil, habbilim, hakkol habil!* quoth Mr Bloom. (I had the words written for me by him that I might astonish my Friends with my Hebraic Learning.) 'But while we are speaking of the Greeks,' said Mr Crawley, 'I have a mind to repeat a Poem of such beauty that it seems to me to be the still small Voice itself after the Thunder and Lightning of Greek Tragedy. Now, My God,' he cried, striking the marble table with his handkerchief, 'this is true Poetry –
    "Becalm'd the Sea-gull riding the purple wave ..." '
Uncle became impatient of so much Classical Learning and he inquir'd of Mr Bloom if he were acquainted with the Literature of To-Day. 'I have in my possession', said Mr Bloom, 'some Thousand Volumes bound very exquisite in saffron leather which are uncut and reposing on my Shelves, until I shall have Time to tear myself from my Researches. At present I am engag'd upon the study of Chinese Literature that I may find a certain Word which is known to exist – it is referr'd to by at least one Spanish Chronicler – as expressing the Delight in Sensual Enjoyment as understood by the Squami Monks BC 497 or 8. Failing to find it within a Year I purpose journeying to Berlin, where I am entitl'd to an entry to the Secret Library of the German Emperor. It is possible – *mais pas probable* – that it may be there!' ... By that time, my dear Isabel, I was quite exhausted by all this fine Talk, and I dosed off in my Chair while the gentlemen discours'd of Shaxpere and the Open Vowel ... I am afraid you will not have read thus far. If I might flatter my poor Powers of Relating that you have done so I would send my very best Love to everybody. I have a great deal more to say, but I have no more time at present.

Most affect^{ly},
VIRGINIA

Index